STUDIES IN FRENCH LITERATURE No. 22

General Editor
W. G. Moore
Fellow and Tutor of St. John's College, Oxford

STENDHAL:

LE ROUGE ET LE NOIR

by

JOHN MITCHELL

Lecturer in French, University of Southampton

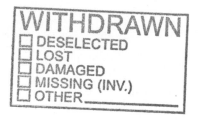

EDWARD ARNOLD

© JOHN MITCHELL 1973

First published 1973
by Edward Arnold (Publishers) Ltd.
25 Hill Street, London W1X 8LL

Cloth edition ISBN: 0 7131 5670 8
Paper edition ISBN: 0 7131 5671 6

Printed in Great Britain by
The Camelot Press Ltd, London and Southampton

Contents

Acknowledgements

The Publishers' thanks are due to Garnier Frères, Paris, for permission to reproduce extracts from *Le Rouge et le Noir* by Stendhal in the Classiques Garnier edition, edited by Henri Martineau.

1. Modes

Expansion. That is the idea the novelist must cling to. Not completion. Not rounding off but opening out. (E. M. Forster)

There is no easy formula to define the ever-widening appeal of *Le Rouge et le Noir*. It moves in many modes and calls up echoes of many forms; it presents many aspects of reality and suggests a variety of ways of considering them. To attempt to confine the author's vision within any single one of them, to consider the novel as a tract for this or that political, philosophical or literary creed, is to distort and ossify. If we are to accept the novel at all, we must accept the multiplicity of its paradoxes—its irony and its passion, its concern for political responsibility and its unworldly idealism, Julien's freedom in imprisonment, his success and his failure, Mathilde's grandiloquent final gesture and our certainty of the truth of Julien's prediction that she will forget him and live normally, that same gesture and the adjacent notation of Madame de Rênal's quiet death, a death which is at once implausible and aesthetically right—all these and many other paradoxes we must accept as equally valid, in order to see that the truth about Stendhal's vision lies, not in any one of these points, but somewhere above the centre of the interlocking tensions which exist within and between them. This synthesis is itself paradoxical; it is complete and cohesive, but at the same time provokes the reader to continue to crystallize after he has closed the book, leaving him in that state of free-roaming rêverie which Stendhal considered to be the greatest power of all art.

Looking thus upon his masterly reconciliation of apparent incongruities, we can apply to Stendhal the epithet of 'comprehensive soul' which, after Dryden, he was wont to apply to his beloved Shakespeare. In this sense we can call his achievement that of a poet. 'What is a poet?' asks Coleridge in his *Biographia Literaria*:

He diffuses a tone and spirit that blends and, as it were, fuses [the faculties] each into each by that synthetic and magical power to which I would exclusively appropriate the name of imagination. This power reveals itself in the balance or reconcilement of discordant qualities.

If *Le Rouge* is one of the great prose epics, is it not because in its pages a wide variety of moods are contained, controlled and given unity by the unmistakeable voice of the author? Its peculiarly lucid ambiguity is evident in a bare summary of the events involving the central character, who is alternately mocked and admired by his author. Julien Sorel is both hero and rascal, a cunning *ingénu*, ruthless and hypersensitive, a timid upstart rooted in the vain and hypocritical society whose values he despises and whose barriers his class-consciousness annihilates. Seducing two women to further his ends but caught in the snare he lays for them, this ambitious schemer succeeds, recklessly throws everything away, finds happiness in prison with the woman he has tried to kill and, hungering for life, faces death with serenity. Here indeed are 'quelques faits qui jettent un jour singulier sur les profondeurs du cœur humain.' (*Chroniques Italiennes*, I, p. 3.)[1]

Stendhal succeeds here in reconciling the demands of three principal types of prose fiction. Firstly, *Le Rouge* has all the characteristics of a major conventional novel, in which the author uses mimetic means to present credible, complex individuals living in a recognizable place and society, and involved in plausible events in a story with a clear shape, moving through a climax to a change in situation and a regrouping of relationships. It also presents a probing psychological portrait of the hero and of certain other characters, using techniques which foreshadow the stream of consciousness.

Secondly, an important function of the work—implied by the subtitle *Chronique de 1830*—is to reconstruct an anatomy of that society, using predominantly satirical or comic methods aimed both at institutions and at individual characters in so far as they are products of their society. Not even the hero is exempted from this satirical presentation.

Finally, the work contains strong elements of romance; we are ultimately invited to consider the hero *in vacuo* and to envisage his story as a quest which culminates in the attainment of the unattainable. Moreover, parallels are established with models drawn from both history and literature—but in either case considered as myths—which are at once idealized and confronted with the author's own ideal, and eventually replaced by it. The structure of values in the novel is an exploration of an ideal, which is achieved, found wanting, overthrown, and replaced by an even higher one, which is also briefly achieved.

---

[1] For details of all editions of Stendhal's work referred to, see page 36.

VIEWPOINT

If there is one gift more essential to a novelist than another it is the power of combination—the single vision. (Virginia Woolf)

If there is such diversity of mood in the book, how is its distinctive unity achieved? Is it through the presence of the hero? He originally gave his name to the title, which was changed only shortly before publication. The meaning of the final title has been much disputed. Most plausible is the common view that the colours represent respectively the uniforms of the military career Julien would have liked and the ecclesiastical one he considers more prestigious in 1830. The other varying interpretations[2] need not be mutually exclusive, but perhaps *Julien* is after all the most appropriate title for a novel so completely dominated by a hero so favoured by his author. Julien is the pivot of all Stendhal's approaches to his material; he is at the focal point of all the relationships; he both causes and is affected by all the action; he is, in his role of innocent at large, a major agent of the satire; he is the discoverer of the values towards which the whole work tends.

And yet we cannot say that he gives the book its unity, for sometimes he is absent, physically or mentally. Often he must share the centre of our attention, notably with Mathilde, sometimes to the extent of taking second place—at the ball where we begin to see for the first time into Mathilde's thoughts (II, Chs. 8 and 9). Occasionally, he must even play a subsidiary role to a comic minor character, as happens at Strasbourg (II, Ch. 24) and in the ensuing chapters, where his behaviour continues to be dominated by the fatuous Korasoff. When he prowls about the de la Mole garden, armed to the teeth and shaking with fright, before climbing the ladder to Mathilde's bedroom, he is certainly at the centre of the action since he is alone, but he appears here detached in a comic light; hence, though we still see the action through his eyes, it is not through his consciousness that we judge it. Sometimes he is simply not there, for reasons of plausibility—as when Pirard arranges for him to become the Marquis de la Mole's secretary, or when the Marquis wonders what steps to take about Mathilde's pregnancy, or when M. de Rênal broods on the anonymous letter denouncing his wife's adultery.

If the hero's presence is not sufficient to explain the unity of the book, it is because we are, above and beyond this, aware of the presence of

[2] For a full survey see P. G. Castex, *Le Rouge et le Noir de Stendhal* (Paris, S.E.D.E.S., 1967), pp. 18–22.

the author's consciousness. Julien's most significant absence occurs at the beginning; he does not appear at the centre of the narration until the fifth chapter. Stendhal does not share his hero's view of the world; he is inventing, not confessing. He may have considerable sympathy, but he always leaves himself a certain critical margin, his right to which is established by this delayed entry.

FOCUS

A novelist can shift his view point if it comes off. Indeed this power to expand and contract perception . . . has a parallel in our perception of life. (E. M. Forster)

Certainty about the point of view from which we witness the events is essential in providing a sense of unity to the novel. In *Le Rouge* we are never in doubt about where—physically—we are placed to witness a scene, or how—morally, emotionally, intellectually—we are asked to judge it. The sharp focus and intense immediacy of scenes like the ceremony at Bray-le-Haut (I, Ch. 18) are partly due to the recurrent indications of the angle and range of Julien's view of the events:

> Le roi entra. Julien eut le bonheur de le voir de très près. . . . Le chœur était environné de stalles, et les stalles élevées de deux marches sur le pavé. C'était sur la dernière de ces marches que Julien était assis. . . . Julien était à six pas du roi. . . . Il remarqua, pour la première fois, un petit homme au regard spirituel. . . . Julien remarqua qu'il y avait sur l'autel des cierges qui avaient plus de quinze pieds de haut. . . . Ce fut alors seulement que Julien, collé contre la porte dorée, aperçut, par-dessous le bras nu d'une jeune fille, la charmante statue de saint Clément.

Julien is the observer whose presence authenticates the narrative. But the observer is also observed. His judgement of events often coincides with his author's, yet there are recurrent reminders of his inadequacy, his ingenuousness, his prejudices, and the limits of his comprehension. The author's judgement of events remains superior to the hero's. We are never in doubt as to what judgements Stendhal wishes us to make, though he rarely forces his opinions upon us, avoiding dogmatism through continual variations of tone and pace—moments of suspense, emotion, irony, seriousness, comedy, mystery, lucidity follow one another in unending succession.

To demonstrate the flexibility of tone which goes to make up the unity of vision, one can, ultimately, only refer the reader back to the novel, or at most ask him to consider the range of implications which Stendhal makes from one basic fact of the plot. M. de Rênal's decision to get a tutor for his children provides a whole series of insights: satirical ones into Rênal's status-seeking vanity, Sorel's greed and cunning, and Valenod's vulgarity; delicately compassionate ones into Madame de Rênal's naïve gentleness; and a whole gamut into Julien's complex and tempestuous nature, ranging from the fragile beauty of his first meeting with Madame de Rênal to the high comedy of his recitation of Latin to M. de Rênal's gaping servants, Rousseau giving place to Molière within one chapter (I, Ch. 6).

It is perhaps with this in mind that critics have made analogies with cinematic technique,[3] for we are always aware of seeing the events as though through the lens of a camera operated by a director expert in shifting the angle of vision. Because the shifts are continual, we grow accustomed and do not feel disorientated or bewildered—except when the author wishes it, as in the Secret Note episode in Part II. We pass from angle to angle so rapidly and fluidly that we do not notice the shifts until they have taken place, and by then we have moved on again. This amalgam of different perspectives, in a scene such as Julien's first meeting with Madame de Rênal, where we see events now through one person's eyes, now through the other's, now from the outside, now in close-up, presents a many-sided reality. We see its various planes, but selectively, and in sharp focus.

However varied and fluid this shifting of narrative angle may be, it does reveal a dominant pattern—a movement from the outside inwards. We begin with the distant view, and move into ever more detailed close-up; we are asked to perceive scenes through sense-impressions before being invited to judge them; we pass from bewilderment to understanding, from irony to sympathy, from logic to passion. This tendency towards an ever deeper involvement on the part of author and reader is no doubt the proper movement of the novel. When we first open the book, the author is a stranger who must observe the forms of politeness and modesty; by the end, he is at least a close acquaintance. He may, if he has managed to win our confidence, have become a friend, whose concerns are our concerns. He will only have done so if he has

[3] For instance Georges Blin, in *Stendhal et les problèmes du Roman* (Paris, J. Corti, 1954).

begun by treating us with respect. Stendhal's awareness of the author's duty to avoid insulting his reader's intelligence is at the root of his life-long preoccupation with the problem of style.

STYLE

The whole secret of a living style lies in not having too much style. (Thomas Hardy)

In an age when an effusive and inflated manner of writing was the fashion, Stendhal was almost alone in realizing that style is not merely a decoration, that it concerns not simply the more or less pretty arrange-ment of words but the whole manner in which the narration is presented. Consideration of it is therefore central to any discussion of his work, and not merely to be tagged on as an afterthought.

In his four drafts of a reply to Balzac's generous article on *La Chartreuse de Parme*,[4] Stendhal accepts many suggestions as to the restructuring of the novel, but is adamant in defence of his style, indicating quite clearly that he had constantly been at pains to render it as simple and unemotive as possible:

> Je suis d'accord sur tout excepté sur le style. . . . Le style ne saurait être trop clair, trop simple . . . pour prendre le ton, je lisais de temps en temps quelques pages du Code Civil. (*Correspondance*, III, pp. 394–403)

He obviously attached considerable importance to this whole question, reflecting on it throughout his career and reaching some very precise conclusions. If we tend not to notice the style when we are reading *Le Rouge*, whilst at the same time being constantly aware of a highly individual tone of narration, this is a measure of Stendhal's success in conforming to the criteria which emerge particularly from the studies he made, between 1812 and 1815, of the style of various French writers.

The epitome of good style for Stendhal would be best described by his favourite word *naturel*. Firstly, the tone of narration should be conversa-tional and unobtrusive:

> Le style doit être comme un vernis transparent: il ne doit pas altérer les couleurs, ou les faits et les pensées sur lesquels il est placé. (*Mélanges de Littérature*, III, p. 98)

[4] See Balzac, *Œuvres Complètes* (Paris, Conard, 1940) XL, pp. 371–405.

Secondly, the writer must be true to himself, so that we can instantly recognize him in his writing:

> Première de toutes les règles de style laquelle est sans exception: être soi-même. . . . On dit qu'un homme a un style, lorsque, rencontrant une phrase, on peut dire qu'elle est de lui. (*Ibid.*, p. 93)

As usual, there is something of a paradox here. The writer is asked to be at once noticeable and unnoticeable. The theory poses two contradictory ideals; in practice, Stendhal succeeds without difficulty in adhering to both of them, effecting a reconciliation which is perhaps clarified by taking a closer look at those early studies.

The first contention is that style should be unobtrusive, that the writer should state the facts of the narration without interposing his own reaction to them. The ideal is well expressed in the contrast between Stendhal's admiration for the cool, self-effacing style of Fénelon and his mistrust of the intrusive and intoxicating manner of Rousseau:

> Le style de Fénelon décrit les choses, et non pas la situation de son âme en les voyant. (*Ibid.*, p. 97)
>
> Rousseau nous dit de chaque chose ce que nous devons en penser. (*Ibid.*, p. 114)

Stendhal argues this preference on several grounds. In the first place, Fénelon's style allows a greater flexibility of mood, from the comic all the way through to the tragic, whereas Rousseau's constantly emotive manner rules out the possibility of comedy. Secondly, the cool style avoids the problems of inflation; big words and poetic images, through being rarely used, retain their value and can therefore create their full and precise effect when needed. This explains Stendhal's sparing use of adjectives in *Le Rouge*. Thirdly, a too consciously poetic style runs the risk of alienating the reader by diverting his attention from the content. As Stendhal says in his letter to Balzac:

> Je ne veux pas branler l'âme du lecteur. Ce pauvre lecteur laisse passer les mots ambitieux, par exemple *le vent qui déracine les vagues*, mais ils lui reviennent après l'instant de l'émotion. (*Correspondance*, III, p. 402)

Whilst we are pausing to marvel at the ingenious strangeness of a word, we have ceased to be involved; the novel has become a thing to be admired instead of a means of communication.

Finally, the neutral style protects the author from the ridicule which greets the failure of a too obvious attempt at emotivity. Of Fénelon he says: 'Le cœur froid qui ne sympathise pas avec lui ne peut lui donner un ridicule' (*Mélanges de Littérature*, III, p. 97). If on the other hand the author says, 'What I am about to tell you is very moving' (for example the opening pages of *Le Père Goriot*) and then fails to move us—and the fact of his telling us will have reduced his power to convince the intelligent reader—he will appear ridiculous and undermine his future authority.

This awareness of the vulnerability of the man who undertakes to publish the secrets of his imagination is crucial in determining Stendhal's style and its effect on the reader. His circumspection, his refusal to take our amiability for granted, increases our respect for him and hence engages our willingness to enter freely into the illusion he offers. It is above all our freedom—to be moved or bored as we choose—that Stendhal is concerned to preserve:

> Le style de Fénelon, ne nous disant pas ce que nous devons éprouver, nous abandonne à notre faculté de sentir, il laisse les tièdes dans leur froideur. . . . Nous sommes libres d'en penser ce que nous voudrons. (*Ibid.*, p. 112)

No special pleading; reality is to be presented without comment or distortion—'La vérité, l'âpre vérité', Stendhal reminds himself in the epigraph to *Le Rouge*. For a man endowed with an intense sensitivity, truth is only to be found by rigorously silencing the solipsistic promptings of the heart and stating no more than is proveable. Chapter IX of *De l'Amour*, that work of confessional therapy of 1821, provides a revealing insight into the restraints which Stendhal imposes upon himself when writing:

> Je fais tous les efforts possibles pour être *sec*. Je veux imposer silence à mon cœur qui croit avoir beaucoup à dire. Je tremble toujours de n'avoir écrit qu'un soupir quand je crois avoir noté une vérité.

Emotionalism is suspect; only facts do not lie—hence Stendhal's choice of a *fait divers* for the basis of his novel. The account of the trial of Antoine Berthet in the *Gazette des Tribunaux* of December 1827 reads very much like a summary of *Le Rouge*. Berthet was a young man of humble birth from the small town of Brangues in Isère. Exceptionally bright, he became the protégé of the local *curé* and went to a seminary, which he fairly soon left, supposedly for health reasons. He returned to Brangues to become tutor to the children of a M. Michoud de la Tour, and eventually the lover of M. Michoud's previously virtuous wife.

Later, he went to the seminary at Grenoble; again he left, to become tutor to the children of a M. Cordon, and this time had an affair with his employer's daughter. Betrayed by a letter from Madame Michoud, dismissed again, he shot Madame Michoud during Mass in the parish church at Brangues, was tried, condemned, and executed in February 1828.

That this was the principal source of *Le Rouge*, along with a similar case involving a man called Lafargue,[5] is beyond doubt, since Stendhal all but confirms it in a letter to Count Salvagnoli in 1831. That the novel had such a source is interesting as one example of Stendhal's need of a catalyst to his imagination, some strange and striking sequence of events which aroused in him a productive curiosity about the peculiarities of human behaviour. More pertinently, it demonstrates his need for an external discipline, some basic structure to which he can point with absolute certainty and say that all this actually happened. The task which then remains to him as novelist is to give shape and meaning to the untidiness of reality, to provide the transitions between the given events, to ask his imagination and experience what circumstances, what characteristics of the persons involved might have motivated such behaviour, and what effect the events might in turn have had on these persons.

Stendhal's deep concern for checking the findings of his imagination by reference to fact is demonstrated by his retrospective validation of the dénouement when, in his own copy of the published novel, he made a marginal note by the sentence 'Julien était parti pour Verrières' (p. 449), in which he indicated the analogy between this scene and an episode which befell Berlioz in 1831. This episode, recounted with delightful self-mockery in the *Mémoires* which Berlioz wrote much later on, concerns his reaction to a letter which he received in Florence from the mother of his mistress, Camille Moke, informing him of her daughter's impending marriage to his friend Pleyel. Enraged, he set off for Paris with the intention of shooting everyone concerned, including himself. Fortunately, by the time he got as far as Nice—a journey, be it noted, no shorter than Julien's from Paris to Verrières—he came to his senses, and the planned mayhem never happened. Whilst the journey lasted, he was totally obsessed by his passion, yet within the terms of that passion he acted with cool deliberation, spending quite some time in Genoa fitting

[5] For a study of the importance of this source, see Claude Liprandi, *Au cœur du Rouge, L'affaire Lafargue et Le Rouge et le Noir* (Lausanne, Grand Chêne, 1961).

himself out with women's clothes so that he could arrive in Paris in disguise. This episode sheds considerable light on the dénouement of *Le Rouge*; above all, the fact that Stendhal himself refers to it reveals the extent of his concern for substantiating his narration with facts.

What is a novel if not a . . . form of imagined life clearer than reality and whose accumulated verisimilitude of selected episodes puts to shame the pride of documentary history? (Joseph Conrad)

Facts from outside the novel; details within it. The meaning of Stendhal's definition of the novel—'un miroir que l'on promène sur la grande route'—which appears twice in *Le Rouge*, is perhaps made clearer by setting it alongside the superficially similar remark made by Balzac in the *Avant-Propos* to the *Comédie Humaine*, where he states that his aim is to create 'un fresque de la société, la saisissant dans l'immensité de ses agitations'. Both use a broadly pictorial analogy; but where Balzac's image emphasizes the immensity of the picture and suggests something fixed and static, Stendhal's implies a greater concern with the *agitations*. It is a mirror which moves—a hand-held camera, to return to our cinematic analogy—and therefore reflects, not a formalized abstraction of reality, but a continuous procession of particular facts, the *petits faits vrais* of which Stendhal was so fond. 'Tout ce qui est vague est faux' (*Marginalia*, I, p. 330); unapplied generalities have no impact on the reader; effects are created only if many details are given, details which on their own may seem insignificant and irrelevant, but which gain both relevance and significance through accumulation. This is surely what Stendhal meant when he wrote:

Car le style est ceci: 'Ajouter à une pensée donnée toutes les circonstances propres à produire tout l'effet que doit produire cette pensée'. (*Mélanges de Littérature*, III, p. 110)

Thus the *pensée donnée* at the beginning of Chapter 25 of Part I might be: 'Julien arrived at the seminary full of terror and a grim sense of foreboding.' To express this, the good story-teller will put us in Julien's skin as he arrives and let us notice all the details of the place as they strike him in his overwrought state: the cross on the door, the echoing bell, the delay in answering, the porter's sinister face, the rickety staircase, the bare walls, the sticking door, the low ceiling, the poor light, the dearth of furniture, the dirty windows, the ill-kept vase of flowers, the angry-looking man scribbling on scraps of paper. He will accumulate the images and words evocative of death, decay, darkness, and rebarbative austerity, and if he does all this well, we shall perhaps be ready to faint with Julien when Pirard finally speaks—or at any rate to laugh sympathetically.

Therefore, whatever objectivity the author may pretend, the famous mirror will be selective, reflecting the significant details chosen to create a narrative effect, the typical anecdote to clinch a point. But if they are carefully chosen, they can be given without comment to the reader, providing him with a framework and a catalyst for his imagination, just as the original source-material provided them for the author's imagination. In both cases the process is similar to the one for which Stendhal invented the word *cristallisation* in *De l'Amour*. There, to explain what happens when a man falls in love, he uses the analogy of a bare branch thrown into the salt-mines; when it is recovered some months later, its appearance is transformed by a myriad glittering crystals. Thus the image of the loved one is thrown into the mind of the lover, who then uses his imagination to embellish it with all the many characteristics he would like to see there. The essence of this idea is the recognition of the omnipotence of the imagination; it is this which makes the analogy relevant to both the conception and the narration of the novel. It is conceived in Stendhal's mind as the result of his imagination embellishing the data of the Berthet affair; it is created in the reader's mind as the result of his imagination elaborating on the clues which the author has planted.

Stendhal provides clues; he shows rather than tells the reader. The *pensée donnée* is not stated explicitly. The author does not say, 'Julien despised the guests at Valenod's dinner-party', or 'Julien and Mathilde were acutely embarrassed when he climbed into her bedroom', or 'Julien was furious on reading Madame de Rênal's letter'; instead he shows us that contempt, that embarrassment, that fury. More than that, he invites us to share it, to lend ourselves to it, and he does this best by showing us the circumstances relating to it. As he wrote to Madame Jules Gaulthier in 1834:

Ne jamais dire: 'La passion brûlante d'Olivier pour Hélène.' Le pauvre romancier doit tâcher de faire croire à la passion brûlante, mais ne jamais la nommer. (*Correspondance*, II, p. 643)

Stendhal repudiates the sterile view of the work of fiction as a beautiful object which the author hands to the reader to admire. He recognizes that the novel is a two-way process, something which happens in the

B

reader's mind, partly as a result of the author's words, partly as a result of the reader's intellectual make-up and of his experience, actual or potential. This recognition is central to his conception of narrative style, and further explains his circumspection towards the reader. What he writes is at best a powerful suggestion to stir our imagination:

> Un roman est un archet; la caisse du violon *qui rend les sons*, c'est l'âme du lecteur. (*Vie de Henry Brulard*, p. 150)

This explains the paradox with which we began. If the first rule of style is *être soi-même*, the author cannot be absent from the novel. He is there, but the reader is there with him, and each one's presence is essential to the other. We need him to manipulate the violin-bow; the most we can ask is that he do it discreetly, at least until he has won our confidence.

Our doctrine is, that the author and the reader should move along together in full confidence with each other. (Anthony Trollope)

Stendhal does intervene continually; the *vernis* of style is not always transparent. He intervenes most obviously with direct comments on his characters and their behaviour. Occasionally this jars, as in the explanation of Julien's reaction to his surroundings on his arrival at the seminary:

> L'émotion et la terreur de Julien étaient telles, qu'il lui semblait être sur le point de tomber. Un philosophe eût dit, peut-être en se trompant: c'est la violente impression du laid sur une âme faite pour aimer ce qui est beau. (p. 169)

This fails through being too overt, but above all through being superfluous. Stendhal has for once not trusted his powers of evocation. It is ironical that this lapse should occur here, since it follows one of the most vividly evocative passages in the novel. Direct intervention works best when it adds a new perspective to the presentation of a character, or reveals an aspect of that character which it would be impossible to reveal in any other way. The comment on M. de Rênal—'Mais laissons ce petit homme à ses petites craintes' (p. 148)—adds little new to our understanding of the character; some of the many comments on Julien are already more useful:

> ... il entreprenait de juger la vie avec son imagination. Cette erreur est d'un homme supérieur. (p. 358)

Il était encore bien jeune; mais, suivant moi, ce fut une belle plante. Au lieu de marcher du tendre au rusé, comme la plupart des hommes, l'âge lui eût donné la bonté facile à s'attendrir. (p. 460)

These come to correct a possibly unfavourable impression of Julien, retrospectively excusing his behaviour. They are comments which need to be made; at the points in the story at which they occur, they cannot plausibly—nor indeed so forcibly—be made by another character, and they are clearly outside the perspective of Julien's self-analysis.

It is with Madame de Rênal that these direct judgements are most frequent and of most value. Often they consist simply of a subjective epithet dropped in passing: 'la pauvre femme' (p. 65), 'la douceur inaltérable de son caractère' (p. 89), 'cette mère malheureuse' (p. 116). Sometimes there is a fuller explanatory comment:

Aucune hypocrisie ne venait altérer la pureté de cette âme naïve. (p. 66)

La pureté de l'âme, l'absence de toute émotion haineuse prolongent sans doute la durée de la jeunesse. (p. 78)

C'était une de ces âmes nobles et romanesques, pour qui apercevoir la possibilité d'une action généreuse, et ne pas la faire, est la source d'un remords presque égal à celui du crime commis. (p. 154)

Sometimes there is abandonment of all pretence at neutrality; after quoting a generalization by a hypothetical philosopher on the likelihood of the nineteenth century, because of its boredom, predisposing all but 'les âmes sèches' to love-affairs, Stendhal adds, 'la réflexion du philosophe me fait excuser Mme. de Rênal' (p. 155).

The direct comments on Madame de Rênal always tend to excuse and ennoble her, and are indispensable. Of all the major characters, she is the one most in need of corrective explanation. Firstly, in spite of having given her attitudes—towards religion, for instance—which are alien to him, Stendhal clearly finds her completely admirable; secondly, she is the character least given to self-analysis and the least conscious of her own admirable qualities, which might pass unnoticed were they not pointed out to us. It is precisely this unpretentious innocence which makes her the most admirable character.

In general, Stendhal's direct interventions tend to serve as footnotes to the narration, illuminating rather than controlling it. They enhance rather than undermine the plausibility of the work by emphasizing the author's separateness from its characters, who could, it is implied, have acted otherwise; it is the author's duty to report the truth, however strange or unpalatable. Thus, Stendhal gives the impression of increasing the characters' freedom from his control, and hence the illusion of their real existence.

On other occasions the interventions are ironic. Particularly distinctive is the double-sided irony Stendhal often employs to protect his emotional vulnerability by appearing to side with the supposedly cynical, worldly-wise reader whenever he wishes to present some idea very close to his heart. This is an extension of Stendhal's basic principle that the reader's amiability should not be taken for granted. Perhaps the most striking example occurs where Julien, decorating the cathedral at Besançon, already somewhat exalted by physical exhaustion as well as by the beauty of the place and the smell of incense, hears the bells begin to ring. He ought, says Stendhal, to be wondering how long it will be before the ropes and beams need replacing, how much it is costing to pay the bell-ringers, what economies can be made, whether the financial outlay is justified in terms of the number of people it draws into the fold. In the middle of this appear these pungent lines:

> Au lieu de ces sages réflexions, l'âme de Julien, exaltée par ces sons si mâles et si pleins, errait dans les espaces imaginaires. Jamais il ne fera ni un bon prêtre, ni un grand administrateur. Les âmes qui s'émeuvent ainsi sont bonnes tout au plus à produire un artiste. (p. 193)

This sort of procedure is very cunning; the reader is either taken in by the irony and nods sagely in agreement, or sees through the ironic mask and wins admission to the 'happy few', that unspecified élite to whom *Le Rouge*, along with other works of Stendhal, is dedicated.

Stendhal also intervenes—as must any author—by the nature of his selection. Let us remind ourselves of one of his most striking definitions of style: 'Ajouter à une pensée donnée toutes les circonstances propres à produire tout l'effet que doit produire cette pensée'. Most significantly, he then adds: 'On est le maître de choisir ces circonstances, et l'ordre dans lequel on les montre.' One of the innovations in Stendhal's narrative style is his preference for the natural order in the presentation of circumstances—that is, from perception to explanation. Details appear one by one, apparently at random, as they might to an uninformed observer; at first all is baffling; then, as the sense-impressions accumulate, the reader begins to relate them one to another, until understanding dawns. Examples of this procedure include Julien's attendance at the auction in Verrières, his arrival at the seminary, the Secret Note episode, the encounter with the Comte de Beauvoisis's coachman in Paris, and the ceremony at Bray-le-Haut—in particular Julien's meeting with the Bishop of Agde. In this scene (p. 104) Julien, searching for the Bishop, comes into a large room of faded grandeur, and then, through his innocent eye, we are given a series of sense-impressions: there is a mirror; there is a young man in front of it; he is in ecclesiastical robes; he looks cross; he is repeatedly making the sign of the blessing at his own reflection; he is wearing the pectoral cross. Initial surprised comprehension on the part of Julien—this is the Bishop. Still a mystery remains however; is this some strange preparatory ceremony? Julien brings the mitre; the Bishop is still mechanically blessing himself; when he stops, he also stops looking cross; he is concerned about the angle at which he wears his mitre; he begins to bless himself again.

> C'est clair, dit Julien, osant enfin comprendre, il s'exerce à donner la bénédiction. (p. 106)

Stendhal has here achieved several things at once with tremendous economy. He has created suspenseful interest, he has given the scene immediacy, he has helped us to get to know the witness—here, as so often, the hero—by placing us in his consciousness, and he has provided a satirical comment on the Bishop, the clergy, and the difficulties of public life. He has also allowed us to feel comically detached from the hero-witness, since we, divining the Bishop's vanity through his rather touching anxiety, have reached comprehension a little ahead of Julien.

The ultimate in selection is total omission and silence, and it is to these that Stendhal resorts at the climactic moments. At the climaxes of action —the ladder-climbing, the encounter in Besançon cathedral, the shooting—primacy is given to the relation of facts. Only what is absolutely relevant is mentioned; there is little comment or explanation beyond that implied by the juxtaposition of details in taut, terse phrases. Stendhal achieves at such moments a rapid heightening of tension and an intense sharpening of focus. At the climaxes of emotion a different type of restraint is used. Stendhal's refusal to indulge in any special pleading for the sake of engaging our emotional sympathy is intensified to the point of almost total withdrawal from the narration at precisely those moments when he wishes to involve us most. In *Vie de Henry Brulard*, the partial autobiography written five years after *Le Rouge*, Stendhal spends several stammering pages of his final chapter trying to explain how and why he was so intensely happy during his first visit to Milan in 1801, before finally abandoning the attempt on the grounds that 'le sujet dépasse le disant'. This honest realization of the limitations of his craft, of the inability of words to do justice to big emotions, is turned to advantage in moments such as Julien's execution, which, after the briefest of nostalgic references to Vergy, is narrated in a single sentence which describes its own exemplary dignity and restraint:

> Tout se passa simplement, convenablement, et de sa part sans aucune affectation. (p. 506)

By saying even less than he quite legitimately could, Stendhal makes us all the more aware of what is left unsaid and, shunning his own by no means meagre stylistic resources, throws us instead on to the even richer resources of our own imaginative empathy.

Stendhal's narrative style appeals to the intelligence and imagination, and depends on an actively cooperative reader, prepared to crystallize around the author's clues, but to cooperate freely, to shift his areas of association, to respond now with his head, now with his heart, as and when the author shifts the nature of his appeal. And, as he shifts, he accumulates new perspectives, new perceptions, so that the complete picture emerges only at the end. Hence the powerful impression of lived reality which emanates from the novel, which, like life, consists of an unbroken series of present moments whose relationships are established and given sense by the judgement of a human consciousness working in time through intentions and memory. Indeed, there are two consciousnesses working together, the author's standing like a magic filter in front of the reality which, as it passes through him, acquires a sense which will be completed by the reader in the context of his own experience.

2. Methods

SETTING

Descriptions should be very brief and have an incidental character. One has to snatch at small details. (Anton Chekhov)

The absence of a conventional descriptive technique is one of the most welcome features of *Le Rouge*. We form our mental image of people and places in novels almost in spite of any information the author gives us of visual details. It is always disappointing to see a dramatized adaptation of a book; things and people never look as we had imagined; they are limited in a way the imagined picture is not. Physical description beyond a certain optimum level becomes counter-productive; instead of actively creating with the author, we sit back, our imagination lulled, and passively receive information we are unable to retain.

PLACE

Unlike Balzac, in whose novels the action rarely starts before the place has been firmly and meticulously established, Stendhal assigns a minor role to physical description. What does appear is quick, impressionistic and highly selective—all the more effective for that, since it focuses our attention immediately upon the aspects which the author wishes us to retain, operating like the real-life observer, not devouring every last detail but noting some features sharply, others more vaguely.

However, there is nothing vague or imprecise about the settings. If they are impressionistic, it is because they are presented from a clearly defined human perspective. With Balzac, the stage is massively set almost independently of the human beings who appear on it; with Stendhal, it is only through the minds of the human beings that places are called up. When characters are mentally absent, preoccupied with other matters, place blurs into a mere accompaniment or ceases to exist, or else only the immediately perceptible area remains in sharp focus. Julien and Madame de Rênal, blissfully holding hands in the garden at Vergy, notice nothing of their surroundings but the darkness of the night, the rustle of the wind in the lime-trees, perhaps the distant bark of a dog. When Madame de

Rênal gets up to pick up a vase blown over by the wind, one feels a shock of intrusion by the physical world (p. 54). When she signals to Julien that the crisis provoked by the anonymous letter is at an end, she notices the sound of the birds and cicadas only because they prevent her from hearing Julien's shout, she sees the unbroken green expanse of the tree-tops only because somewhere it hides Julien (p. 131). Amanda Binet leans across the counter in the café in Besançon, and suddenly Julien is aware of nothing beyond her voluptuous figure (p. 163). Shortly afterwards, absorbed in the emotional crisis of his first meeting with Pirard, he only becomes aware as the tension eases that he has been staring at his own luggage for the past three hours (p. 174).

The examples are innumerable, culminating in the church at Verrières where, beyond the view of the back of Madame de Rênal's praying head, Julien's perception of the physical world is limited to the sound of the bell for the beginning of Mass (p. 449). The external world is perceived only as it is relevant to the preoccupied consciousness of one or other of the characters. The result for the reader is a heightened awareness of the character's state of mind and a very intense because clearly limited sense of place.

As well as revealing the characters' state of mind, place is used to influence it, to mirror it, and to comment upon it. The Julien who leaves for Paris at the end of Part I is different from the one who arrived at the seminary a few chapters earlier. Living in an atmosphere of suspicion and slow, patient ambition, he has become more watchful, more sober, more coldly ambitious. After some time in Paris, he is able to hide his emotional turmoil beneath a display of irreproachable efficiency in his work and of inscrutable elegance in his social dealings with a consistency he could never have achieved in his provincial days. The major changes of place in the novel are thus linked not only with changes in Julien's status but also with developments in his character and hence in the plot. Since the plot finally appears to us as a search by the hero—for happiness, for identity—it is inevitable that the action should move from setting to setting, conveying the time-honoured image of a journey. In all these changes of setting, the unforced vitality and spontaneity of country life is frequently contrasted with the elegantly boring artificiality of life in the capital. This contrast is epitomized in the characters of the two heroines and in the nature of Julien's affairs with them—'C'est l'amour de tête comparé à l'amour du cœur', as Stendhal says in his letter to Salvagnoli (p. 525). But this particular contrast only strikes home because it is supported by a subtly created but equally clear contrast in setting.

Stendhal's presentation of Paris is totally lacking in physical description of the city. With the exception of Julien's forays into the de la Mole garden, there are no memorable outdoor scenes in Paris. Unlike Balzac, Stendhal does not accompany his hero as he strolls by the Seine, or rides in the Bois de Boulogne, or walks home through the muddy streets. In the first part of the novel, on the other hand, much that is important occurs out of doors. Our most poignant awareness of the contrast between worldliness and simplicity comes from our memory of the scenes at Vergy, where the pastoral innocence and seclusion of the place both cause and parallel Julien's childlike happiness as he chases butterflies with Madame de Rênal, whilst at the same time they provide an ironic comment upon his blind inability to grasp the full force of this happiness, obsessed as he still is by his class-consciousness. Significantly, the only brief period of genuine mental intimacy between Julien and Mathilde before they have begun to think of one another as lovers—and therefore as enemies—is also given an outdoor setting, as they take to strolling in the garden, deep in artless conversation (pp. 302–4). Afterwards, their relationship will develop around the blue sofa in the stifling atmosphere of the salon, or in the library, or in the bedroom; at best it will move to a more spacious but more emotionally charged indoor setting, at the Opéra or at the ball.

It is interesting to compare the scene at the ball (pp. 281–96) with the scene of the King's visit to Verrières (pp. 98–110), where there was still a strong reliance upon visual impressions; at the ball, there are two or three sentences upon the appearance of the rooms, and then nothing. And yet we are left with an equally vivid impression of a big social occasion with all its large movement and its suppressed undercurrents. Stendhal achieves this by telling us who is there, what they say, what some of them are thinking, who is the centre of attention, who secretly fears or hates whom, what private scandals are being publicly overlooked, how difficult it is to move; in other words, he concentrates our attention on people to create the Parisian settings.

The city is above all the domain of people; naturalness is absent because Nature is absent. The solitary places which console Julien—those dominating glimpses of wide landscapes which recall his secrecy and moral isolation whilst promising him freedom, power and happiness—these are to be found at Vergy, in the mountains where Fouqué lives, in the view from the seminary-cell at Besançon, in the same more extensive view from the citadel. In Paris, Julien is at his most exposed, because there are so many people and nowhere to escape; when he is alone here, he can only look inwards to his own resources. He has already become more self-reliant and blasé through his stay at the seminary, where he was alone for the first time; thus it is right that his arrival in Paris, in strong contrast with his traumatic arrival in Besançon, should make relatively little initial impact on his senses or, through him, on ours.

In the evocation of Verrières at the beginning of the novel the crucial factor is that the hero has not yet been introduced. Once he has, we almost always see places largely through his consciousness. Here lies the author's main opportunity of establishing his own perspective, which he will then remind us of throughout the book in his interventions. What he must do here is to give us the moral picture of the place as it is seen through his attitudes; but if he does only this, he will have created only a caricature of place. He must first win our confidence and convince us of the reality of the place with an appearance of objectivity. Only when he has lifted us out of the world of everyday reality we are in as we start to read the book and placed us firmly into his fictional world can he afford to start divulging his opinions.

He succeeds in this task with remarkable rapidity and economy. By the end of the first chapter we have already moved from the detached view of the place, as seen by the outside visitor, through to a closely committed inside comment on its moral climate. The presentation is admirably brief; in three short paragraphs we are told the geographical location, the temporal setting, the general appearance of the town and its surroundings, and its principal industry. Yet even in the first sentence the words 'peut passer pour', avoiding a more directly dogmatic statement, make us already aware of the imminence of an ironically critical reservation. This impression is reinforced as the pleasing visual aspect of the place shown, as it were, from the air is followed at once by the unpleasant shock of the noise which greets us as we come down to earth and enter the town. Strokes of irony accumulate through the impressionistic sketch of the apparently self-important mayor, through the anecdote concerning his bad bargain with Sorel, until by the end of the first short chapter the author's scorn for the character of the small French town can burst forth in an overt if as yet enigmatic comment:

La tyrannie de l'opinion, et quelle opinion! est aussi bête dans les petites villes de France qu'aux États-Unis d'Amérique. (p. 6)

By the time the hero enters, halfway through the fourth chapter, many of the major themes of the first part of the novel have been stated. The tyranny of public opinion, the shadow of Napoleon, the rigid hierarchy of the class-structure, the clandestine power of the clergy, the chicanery, the greed, the vanity, the materialistic indifference to natural beauty—all these characteristics of the French provincial town under the Restoration are hinted at. We have also met or had mention of the hero's father, both his future employers, one of his future mistresses, two of his mentors— Chélan and the chirurgien-major—and two future arch-enemies— Valenod and Maslon. This is typical of Stendhal's method; he prefers not to establish his subject slowly, stage by stage:

> J'aime mieux énoncer d'une manière claire et tranchée la vérité qui est l'objet d'un chapitre et la prouver ensuite successivement. (*Mélanges de Littérature*, III, p. 125)[1]

Thus we get premonitions of future events in the novel. Perhaps it is no accident that one of the first episodes (I, Ch. 3) concerns a visit to the prison where Julien will be taken much later in the novel.

It is certainly no accident that Julien is made to visit the church at Verrières on his way to the Rênal household (pp. 24-25). In view of the details here—the red curtains in the dark church, Julien's emotion, his sitting in the Rênal pew—it is clear that Stendhal is following a convention of the historical novels of Sir Walter Scott by planting omens at the beginning of the hero's career which will prefigure later events, and especially the dénouement. There is, however, a certain irony; it is not M. de Rênal's pew but his marriage-bed that Julien will usurp. Moreover, in the climax of the scene, Stendhal mocks the convention, for Julien's discovery of the scrap of paper referring to the execution of a man whose name is an anagram of his own is so blatantly contrived that it must be tongue-in-cheek. More importantly, this is the first stage in the cumulative preparation of the setting and mood of the dénouement. There are three more memorable scenes in church: the ceremony at Bray-le-Haut (I, Ch. 18), the decorating of Besançon cathedral (I, Ch. 28), and the shooting of Madame de Rênal in this same church at Verrières (II, Ch. 35). On each occasion Stendhal draws our attention to the red drapes and the surrounding gloom and on each occasion Julien is in a highly emotional

---

[1] One idea per chapter; this partly explains the function of the chapter epigraphs. Like Brecht's scenic captions, they also maintain our aesthetic distance by stressing the novel's fictitious nature.

state. At Besançon this state of emotion is suddenly further heightened by the same back view of Madame de Rênal at prayer which he will have when he shoots her. By the time we come to the shooting episode, Stendhal can very rapidly evoke a strong sense of place since we have been there—or somewhere similar in mood—three times already. Thus he is able to concentrate on factual details and to give the narrative the uncluttered speed which is essential at this point.

TIME

The Novel we would rather define as 'a fictitious narrative, differing from the Romance, because the events are accommodated to the modern state of society'.
(Sir Walter Scott)

It is, strictly speaking, impossible to separate the evocation of place from that of time in *Le Rouge*. Stendhal is interested in the moral rather than the physical setting, and though the physical is sometimes seen as an influence upon the moral, more generally it is used as an externalization of it; more important as an influence is the historical setting. One of the main lines of argument in *Racine et Shakespeare*, the manifesto for Romanticism which Stendhal wrote in 1823, is that the political changes wrought by history have a profound effect on the tastes and general culture of a country, that what was appropriate under a system of absolute monarchy is no longer relevant or acceptable to a country which has had a republic. The years between 1789 and 1830, when *Le Rouge* was published, are arguably the most turbulent in the history of France, and it is impossible to exaggerate their effect on Stendhal, who was passionately interested in the events of those years, and even involved at first-hand through his association with Napoleon's administration and army between 1801 and 1813. As he implies in *Racine et Shakespeare*, the experience of the disastrous 1812 campaign alone would have been unsettling enough, but besides this he had seen one political system after another rise, flourish, falter, and fail. This experience leads to a sense of instability, a profound scepticism in the matter of politics, and an equally profound awareness of the way in which the structure of society, and hence the role of the individual, is largely determined by the moment in history. Because it reflects this awareness in a contemporary setting, *Le Rouge et le Noir* is perhaps the first truly historical novel.

It is therefore important to see how Stendhal establishes the historical moment of *Le Rouge* as being uniquely and unequivocally that of the Restoration nearing its climactic end. He can quite simply tell us what the period is by references to recent dates and historical events—'depuis la chute de Napoléon', 'depuis 1815', 'depuis les élections de 182*'; he can refer to contemporary events such as the first performance of *Hernani*; he can mention well-known public figures of the time, or even let them appear with disguised names in the salon of the Marquis de la Mole. All this provides a useful framework, but is not enough to give us the precise feel of the period; for this we need to see attitudes and modes of behaviour. Those announced in the opening chapters are demonstrated throughout the first part of the novel—the touchy vanity of M. de Rênal, the cynical status-seeking of Valenod, the petty greed and hypocritical narrow-mindedness of practically everyone in Verrières and the seminary. But these are characteristics peculiar to a parochial society and are not tied to any specific period. At the most, they can be said to be relatively modern, the attitudes of an aging civilization in which possessions and titles have become a substitute for personal distinction. The contrast with the dynamism of a young civilization is clear when we look at what Stendhal wrote in 1838 with reference to the sixteenth-century chronicle which was to be the main source for *La Chartreuse de Parme*:

> Au 16ème siècle . . . la vanité et le qu'en dira-t-on naissait à peine; et, par exemple, on ne prenait point au sérieux les honneurs décernés par les princes . . . le monde était jeune . . . c'est qu'alors on n'estimait dans un homme que ce qui lui est personnel. (*Mélanges de Littérature*, I, pp. 277–8)

The first half of *Le Rouge* develops the theme of the shoddiness and cramping conformity of life in the provinces; the crucial transitional first chapter of Part II recapitulates it in the conversation between Julien's travelling-companions, Falcoz and St-Giraud. The latter, who in age, circumstances and tastes, seems to bear a close resemblance to Stendhal, clearly blames the present state of affairs on Napoleon—not on Napoleon the brilliant young soldier, but on Napoleon the emperor, corrupted by power and vanity:

> Ton empereur, que le diable emporte . . . n'a été grand que sur les champs de bataille, et lorsqu'il a rétabli les finances avec 1802. Que veut dire toute sa conduite depuis? Avec ses chambellans, sa pompe et ses réceptions aux Tuileries, il a donné une nouvelle édition de toutes les niaiseries monarchiques. Elle était corrigée, elle eût pu passer encore

un siècle ou deux. Les nobles et les prêtres ont voulu revenir à l'ancienne, mais ils n'ont pas la main de fer qu'il faut pour la débiter au public. (p. 230)

Thus, summing up the themes of the first half and looking ahead to those of the second, Stendhal suggests that Napoleon himself, at the height of the *Rouge* of his and France's glory, has laid the foundations for the *Noir*, the long slough of disillusionment, discontent and lack of purpose which followed the national trauma of Waterloo.

The novel abounds in references to Napoleon, but the name alone is not enough to explain our overwhelming awareness of the post-Napoleonic hangover not merely as background but as a vital central element of the novel. This can only be explained by the way in which Stendhal has provided us with a particular, clearly defined focus in Julien's interpretation of his social situation and in the project which he bases on this. From his first appearance it is made clear that Julien is ambitious, and excessively conscious of his humble birth. This is enough to explain why he idolizes Napoleon—Napoleon who was also of relatively humble birth, but who was young and ambitious in a society where there was equality of opportunity, given equality of merit. But those days are over; Julien judges that in his society advancement for a young man of his class is to be gained, not through any open display of personal merit, but through the dark and devious ways of hypocrisy and intrigue. Above all, he judges that, in 1830, with France's military prowess discredited, with the ideals of the Revolution betrayed by Napoleon, with the traditional alliance of Church and absolute monarchy reestablished, the only career whereby a poor plebeian can hope to bypass the class-barriers is in the Church. His project is therefore to be secretive, to pay lip-service to the ideals of the Establishment, to regard everybody as an enemy whose attitudes are dictated by a combination of class-consciousness and the desire for personal gain, and to make it an unshirkable duty to beat this society at its own game.

Through this basic project and through Julien's progress up the social ladder, we are made aware of certain characteristics of this society: the rigid and subtly gradated hierarchy of the class-structure; the clandestine power of the clergy, especially as it is manifested in the Congregation—the Jesuit organization initially founded as an evangelical mission with branches throughout France, now seen by Stendhal[2] as a network of

[2] And by Balzac; see *Le Curé de Tours*.

secret police with lay as well as clerical members seeking to ensure that careers are open only to those who read the approved newspapers and profess the approved opinions; we are made aware of the chicanery of public affairs, of the way in which public office is used for personal gain, and of what we might nowadays call the old school tie syndrome. Above all, we are made aware of a society in which general mutual suspicion is the order of the day, where appearance counts for more than inner reality, and where—as Stendhal says in a phrase usually attributed to Talleyrand—'La parole a été donnée à l'homme pour cacher sa pensée' (p. 136).

This is the present defined in terms of the past; through Julien's nostalgia for the Napoleonic era, a constant comparison is implied. The same comparison is seen from a different angle in the attitudes of the petty nobility in the provinces, and of the aristocracy who frequent the salon of the Marquis de la Mole. They cannot forget that there has already been a revolution, a republic, an egalitarian society, but where Julien remembers this to regret its passing, they do so to fear its return. They know that their right to govern is no longer to be taken for granted, that there might be another revolution, that their heads might roll. Fearing the Napoleon legend, they retreat into rigid and unquestioning absolutism; living on borrowed time, they need to present a united front which precludes any serious discussion of politics. This taboo is lifted only when they believe themselves to be *in camera*, as in the Secret Note episode in Part II, the ultra-royalist conspiracy to engineer an invasion by a foreign power sympathetic to their cause—a conspiracy which, ironically, uses Julien to carry its messages.

The present is also defined by its relationship to the future. The future is particularly uncertain for a society which has lost its sense of purpose and hence of identity, living in a trough following a period of social and political upheaval. There are speculations, however, and while Stendhal, with his distrust of vagueness, gives his novel a very precise historical setting, yet there are parallels and prophecies for our own century. On the first page, with its mention of the saw-mills of Verrières, the manu-facture of calico, and M. de Rênal's ear-splitting nail-factory, there is a hint, fleeting but powerful, of the way in which the Industrial Revolution will change the landscape and character of the small town. Much more sustained is Stendhal's awareness of the associated rise of the bourgeoisie and its materialistic and utilitarian values; 'rapporter du revenu' and 'keeping up with the Joneses'—these are the two great commandments for Rênal, and above all for Valenod, whose wife seems to herald whole regiments of suburban hostesses as she tells her guests the price of every knife, fork and spoon. Equally sustained is the sinister picture of Restoration France as the embryonic totalitarian state, with its secret police, its press-censorship, and its insistence on doctrinaire conformism reinforcing the debilitating effects of the process of civilization on the individual. At the same time, Stendhal points to the anonymous uniformity of this kind of society in order to question the whole basis of democracy in the tyranny of the lowest common factor of public opinion. Also implied are the complex problems involved in the conflict between social values and individual merit, between the need for order and the desire for freedom. That Stendhal ultimately leaves these problems unsolved in no way diminishes the value of his treatment of them. The artist's task is not to propose solutions, but to make us aware of the problems; if they were solved, they would no longer interest us.

SOCIETY

It is the habit of my imagination to strive after as full a vision of the medium in which a character moves as of the character itself. (George Eliot)

Stendhal's profound awareness of the future socio-political implications of his era is complemented by an accumulation of details of contemporary social institutions and pastimes. Revitalizing the Romantic cliché of local colour, he contrives to remain deeply involved in his period whilst finding the detachment which is necessary if he is not simply going to offer us a detailed but unfocused close-up. He achieves this by adopting a basically anatomical or satirical presentation. The satire is wide-ranging, but since satire is above all iconoclastic, it is inevitable that the two objects singled out for particular attention should be the Church and the aristocracy, the two elements of Restoration society which have the common characteristic of unquestioning acceptance of established authority.

Detachment is achieved firstly through frequent ironic interventions. Consider for example, on the subject of the atmosphere in the Hôtel de la Mole, the paragraph which begins:

Tel est encore, même dans ce siècle ennuyé, l'empire de la nécessité de s'amuser que même les jours de dîners, à peine le marquis avait-il quitté le salon, que tout le monde s'enfuyait. (p. 251)

This is striking enough, but the long cumulative sentence which follows, with its list of the subjects of conversation which are taboo, reveals with devastating sarcasm the essential characteristics of aristocratic society— the conspiracy of silence on the all-important topic of the political situation. Their position will not bear close examination, so they refuse to discuss it. They seek to escape from the resulting sense of impotent boredom in various pastimes—brittle gossip, attendance at the Opéra, the ball, riding, reading novels, the cult of foppishness or religiosity, the pursuit of love-intrigues. There is a profound comment on the wilful irresponsibility of substituting these frivolous peripheral activities for the more urgent preoccupations which are being ignored. Nowhere is this point more pungently made than in the conversation on politics between Julien and Altamira at the ball (II, Ch. 9).

The ironic interventions often give the impression of being footnotes to the narrative rather than part of it. On at least one notable occasion Stendhal interrupts the narrative for a comment which is quite explicitly parenthetic. This comes in the middle of an account of Mathilde's operatic behaviour, and Stendhal seems initially to be forestalling any possible criticism of the implausibility of her character by blandly avowing that he would not so insult his society as to pretend that Mathilde is drawn from life. Having thus lulled the worldly-wise reader into lowering his defences, he then stabs home:

> Ce n'est point la prudence qui manque aux jeunes filles qui ont fait l'ornement des bals de cet hiver. (p. 356)

He quickly goes on to suggest that this 'prudence' is largely self-seeking and materialistic and, becoming more overt in his social strictures, indicates that Julien has crucially misread his society by trying to go it alone rather than attaching himself to one of the cliques which trample so ruthlessly over the individual—a vital point which will be taken up later by the Marquis de la Mole. Then comes the definition of the novel as 'un miroir qui se promène sur une grande route', as a prelude to a protestation of innocence by the author, who is only doing his job of reporting what he sees; so brilliantly have the transitions of the argument been handled that we scarcely realize that he is thus adopting a pose diametrically opposite to the one with which he began the parenthesis.

This pose of the impartial chronicler is a particularly useful one for the satirist, and lies behind all those techniques which depend for their effect on an anatomical approach. One such technique is the quasi-statistical accumulation of facts and details, for instance about the Church. In the seminary episode in particular, by mentioning a large number of carefully selected trivia, Stendhal is able to create a picture which needs no further comment. He begins with a statistical analysis of the three hundred and twenty-one seminarists; how many are pious, how many are conscientious but dull, how many—the smallest number—are intellectually gifted, how many—the largest number—are simply out to improve their lot (p. 176). Then details begin to appear: the advisability of looking at the ground (p. 179); the properly pious way of eating a boiled egg (p. 180); the slogans on the walls (p. 181)—irresistibly reminiscent of the encouraging thoughts of Chairman Mao; Julien's insensitivity to the privilege of eating *choucroûte* (p. 181); the searching of his luggage (p. 184); his need to defend himself with a pair of compasses (p. 188); his improved prestige among the seminarists after his promotion (p. 197) and after receiving Fouqué's gift of wild boar and venison (p. 198); Frilair's discovery of how to get advancement by filleting the fish of his short-sighted gourmet of a bishop (p. 204). These details, accumulated throughout the book, combine to lay bare the inner workings of the Church as Stendhal sees it. The obligatory ritual acceptance of authority and the outward displays of piety are seen to cover a worldly self-seeking at all levels, from the ruthless opportunist ambition of Frilair down to the modest desire of many of the seminarists to become village-priests as a more comfortable alternative to tilling the soil. The few exceptions to this general stricture—Chélan, Pirard, Chas-Bernard—as well as Stendhal's respectful presentation of Madame de Rênal's sincere faith, make it clear that what he is castigating is not religious belief itself, but the abuse of piety and the excessively important place held by the Church in French political life and in worldly affairs generally.

The religious satire is also applied to the laity, most notably to the sententiously vague religiosity of Madame de Fervaques. In her the satire of the two wings of the Establishment is combined, as she uses her religiosity in three ways: as a means of escape from the prevailing social boredom; as a self-deceptive sublimation of a need for sentimental titillation in her response to Julien's letters; and, in combination with her rank and wealth, as a means to the power to make or break careers in the Church. Julien's dutiful courtship of her is at the centre of much of the satire in the second half of the book. It brings to light the factors just mentioned; it ironically reveals the incompleteness of Julien's opportunism—it never occurs to him that Madame de Fervaques is precisely the person he should cultivate in order to advance not his love-life but his career; it casts a side-light on the foppish absurdity of Korasoff, in accordance with whose mechanistic worldly view of human-beings Julien has undertaken this courtship; it highlights the artificiality of Julien's relationship with Mathilde. More precisely, it is the turning-point in that relationship, which in general is satirically presented through another variation of the anatomical approach—the blow-by-blow analysis, the exhaustive account of all its vicissitudes to the point where we see the two lovers trapped in a machine, driven by wounded vanity, which shuttles them back and forth between desperate longing and contemptuous indifference, only occasionally allowing them to coincide in a sickly frenetic joy.

The comic exaggeration which characterizes many episodes of this affair—for instance, Julien's feats of ladder-scaling, and Mathilde's self-inflicted haircut—is a satirical device particularly evident in Stendhal's character-drawing, and in incidents such as Julien's arrival in the Rênal house (I, Ch. 6), where he recites whole stretches of the New Testament from memory, thus conclusively proving the depth of his piety to the entire gaping household, much as Molière's doctors tend to prove their expertise by reciting meaningless jargon.

Many of these techniques inevitably involve the hero in one way or another; a particularly important use of him as satirical agent is his role of innocent eye, the uninformed outsider travelling through society, viewing it from an alien standpoint and ingenuously commenting upon it. This is a favourite device for the satirist; one thinks of *Gulliver's Travels*, or of *Candide*, or perhaps most pertinently of Montesquieu's *Lettres Persanes*. Particularly striking examples are the ceremony at Bray-le-Haut and the Secret Note episode; in both cases Julien is a lone stranger. These are, however, merely intensifications of the situation throughout the novel; except when he is in prison, Julien is continually moving in a world whose values are foreign to him and, through his impressions of that world, providing the reader with a satirical focus.

Stendhal takes this technique a stage further by a process of ironic reversal in making his hero successfully play society at its own game. The irony is sharpened, and the hollowness of society's values emphasized both by the fact of Julien's detachment from these values and by the manner of his successes. His admission to the seminary and his appointment as secretary to the Marquis de la Mole are unplanned and fortuitous; Madame de Rênal is seduced by his youthful innocence, not by his amorous expertise—as with his final acquisition of wealth and rank, he succeeds in spite of his plans; with Mathilde he succeeds only by following a line of action laid down by somebody else. The accidental nature of these successes deflates Julien's pretensions to cunning, just as the ease of their accomplishment makes a laughing-stock of society's self-supposed shrewdness and confirms Korasoff's mechanistic view of its members, whose response to a given stimulus will always be predictable.

Stendhal's adolescent ambition was 'vivre à Paris en écrivant des comédies' (*Vie de Henry Brulard*, p. 315). To this end he devoted more than half his adult life, systematically analysing plays, passions and dramatic techniques. This rigorous apprenticeship to drama was not wasted on his novels. The influence of Molière is everywhere apparent; the essence of the comedy lies in the fact that the most vulnerable point of the comic character is found precisely where the greatest obsession lies. In *L'Avare* Harpagon is sure to lose his money; in *L'Ecole des Femmes* the more carefully Arnolphe insures against cuckoldry, the more certain he is to be cuckolded; Tartuffe can be gulled only by a blatant charade. The society of *Le Rouge*, epitomized in M. de Rênal, obsessed by vanity and solemnly arming itself with cunning against the fear of ridicule, is deceived and derided by an impetuous bungler.

PEOPLE

You mustn't look in my novel for the old stable ego *of the character.* (D. H. Lawrence)

Stendhal's characters are always capable of surprising us. Our final judgement on them has to be suspended, since throughout the novel they are in a continual process of evolution. Stendhal does not make the mistake of conceiving of character as something static:

J'appelle caractère d'un homme sa manière habituelle d'aller à la chasse au bonheur. (*Vie de Henry Brulard*, p. 314)

This 'chasse au bonheur' is the project which each individual bases on his assessment of his own situation and nature. Thus the basic method of characterization is revelation through behaviour; this means showing not only the acts and speeches of the personages, but also their thoughts and the nature of their relationships.

IMPRESSIONS

I should have thought that my actual characters were described enough to help people to imagine them. However detailed such description is, I am sure that everyone forms his own conceptions, that are different from everyone else's, including the author's. (Ivy Compton-Burnett)

Stendhal does not consider physical details important, except as signs of the inner life. We are not told a great deal about the appearance of the characters. With many of them we are given no physical portrait beyond the highly satisfactory one which our imagination provides on the basis of information about behaviour and attitudes. Where we are given a portrait, it is usually a quick line-drawing rather than a detailed study in heavy oils. As we read the novel, we may forget M. de Rênal's greying hair, broad forehead, aquiline nose and regular features (p. 4), just as we may forget that his wife is tall (p. 13); we may even forget that Julien also has an aquiline nose, as well as chestnut hair and fine irregular features. We do not, however, forget his pale complexion, his lowering brow and his dark eyes, smouldering in the ferocious scowl which so forcibly conveys the grandeur of his discontent from the moment of his first appearance (p. 17). We do not forget the simplicity of Madame de Rênal's manner, the buoyancy of her movements, her youthful grace and vivacity, any more than we forget her husband's self-important strut. The purely accidental physical characteristics are subordinated to those—mainly of movement and expression—which imply the essential manner and attitudes of the character.

Once Julien has become established as the central consciousness, the physical portraits of new characters are always coloured by his state of mind. Arriving at the seminary terrified and oppressed by a sense of ugliness, he notices that Pirard is badly dressed, looks bad-tempered, has a long, blotchy face, a pale forehead, dark eyes and coarse black hair (p. 169). The picture is completely unprepossessing; neither we nor Julien can suspect the depth of sympathy and tenderness which it conceals. Later, when he has come to know him, he will see his honest ugly face among the smiling villains in the de la Mole salon and reflect on the folly of judging by appearances (p. 257). With Mathilde too, Julien's first impression gives little indication of the relationship with her which is to follow. The paucity of detail—'jeune . . . extrêmement blonde et fort bien faite' (p. 242)—conveys Julien's indifference, which hovers on distaste as she reminds him of her mother. His attention is retained only by her eyes, those traditional betrayers of inner secrets. From Julien's reflections on the expression of these eyes, Stendhal leads off into a short but important development, using them to summarize the essence of her character—'L'ennui qui examine, mais qui se souvient de l'obligation d'être important' (p. 243)—and, through Julien's tender memories, to establish a fundamental contrast with Madame de Rênal, whose eyes grow bright, not with the joy of superior wit, but with passion and generosity.

Physical portraits apart, first impressions often provide an important key, since Stendhal usually takes care to present the character in a typical situation or mood. M. de Rênal strolls proprietorially through Verrières, worrying about the threats to his precarious dignity. His wife dutifully listens to him, but is more concerned to watch over the safety of her children. Julien sits in splendid isolation high above the busy centre of his father's sawmill, oblivious of its din, engrossed in reading about Napoleon. Pirard, in austere surroundings, scribbles angrily and submits Julien to a long cross-examination whose rigour relaxes only after Julien has proved his intellectual honesty and his prowess as a Latinist. Our first impression of the Marquis de la Mole precedes his emergence as a major character; throughout the first half of the book, several references and one brief appearance at Bray-le-Haut show him as an influential administrator, impatient and tetchy, attending to his wide range of public and private business. Mathilde's first appearance unremarkably places her at her father's dinner-table, but this is very shortly followed by two significant encounters with Julien, both in the library. On the first occasion she has come illicitly to borrow one of her father's books (p. 246); on the second, she overhears Julien's complaints to Pirard about the tedium of the de la Mole's social evenings (p. 253). Thus Stendhal immediately highlights two important characteristics—her own boredom with the cringing obsequiousness which surrounds her, and her titillating escape from that boredom into the vicarious thrills of literature.

Exposition of character is closely integrated into the action. The formation of Julien's Napoleon-cult through his reading of the *Mémorial de Sainte-Hélène* and the stories of the chirurgien-major, the failure of Madame de Rênal's convent education to prepare her for the realities of married life, the tendency of Mathilde's upbringing to encourage her self-conceit—such essential background information is added piecemeal as the novel proceeds rather than being conveyed in one homogeneous block at the beginning. One senses that Stendhal is creating the character as he writes, and thus allowing us to share in that creation. Once again, there is the sense of a movement inwards; the impressions come first, followed later by the explanation—this is the natural order of events.

It has been said that Stendhal's dialogues are unmemorable. Certainly, he has not Balzac's ear for the rhythms of everyday conversation, but virtuosity in this field would be of little help to the author who wishes to convey the idea of a society dominated by hypocritical conformism, where the main purpose of speech is to conceal thought. In any case, too much concentration on characterization by means of individual speech-patterns can lead to simple caricature, acceptable in minor characters but merely serving to alienate the reader if used persistently for major characters—one thinks of Flaubert's Homais. It is, however, one means used among others by Stendhal, and its contribution is no less effective for being discreet. Mathilde outdoing Molière's Célimène in her malici-ously witty comments on her father's guests, M. de Rênal bluffly generalizing on the unreliable mechanism of women's health, Pirard expressing his affection for Julien with harsh reluctance and talking for preference in Latin—these are the more noticeable idiosyncrasies of speech. Even without such aids to recognition, we are never in doubt in Stendhal's dialogues as to who is talking. This clarity is achieved through precision of viewpoint; we always hear the dialogues through the con-sciousness of one of the characters involved. When, as most often, this is Julien, it frequently happens that we hear directly only what his inter-locutor is saying; his own speeches are summarized indirectly, so that we experience them as he does, noticing their content rather than their form. Moreover, Stendhal always remembers that dialogue involves two people in action and reflects a relationship between characters in tran-sition rather than statically depicting character. It is therefore inter-spersed with references to gestures, facial expressions, tones of voice. Above all, it is illuminated by revelations of thoughts; these more than anything else give solidity to the characters.

THOUGHTS

Much rather would we choose that our readers should clearly understand what our principal actors think, than what they do. (Sarah Fielding)

Stendhal presents characters' thoughts from different perspectives, moving flexibly from one to another, often without transition. Least remarkable is the straightforward summarized report in the author's words. Somewhat more unusual is the use of the *style indirect libre*, which was to become so popular a device for Flaubert and Zola. Here the author borrows the thinker's own words but without attributing them, thus preserving the illusion of his limited knowledge whilst insinuating the character's attitude. Thus, with Valenod thinking of Madame de Rênal:

> Cette femme, la plus distinguée du pays, que pendant six ans il avait environnée de tant de soins, et malheureusement au vu et au su de tout le monde; cette femme si fière . . . venait de prendre pour amant un petit ouvrier déguisé en précepteur. (p. 118)

Often this function is performed by a single subjective word such as the thinker himself might have chosen:

> M. de Rênal, remerciant sa femme, par un sourire, de l'*excellente* idée qu'elle venait d'avoir (p. 13)
> Les enfants l'adoraient, [Julien] ne les aimait point; sa pensée était ailleurs. Tout ce que ces *marmots* pouvaient faire ne l'impatientait jamais. (p. 34) (My italics.)

In the third method, by far the most distinctive, Stendhal moves in even closer and, instead of merely implying the character's words, presents his thoughts directly as a form of inner speech—the interior monologue, as it is usually called. Thought is in reality shapeless, rambling and repetitive, taking a step forward in the inner argument only occasionally as a perception crystallizes. To reproduce such a process verbatim would be both impractical and tedious. Only the salient points of thought appear; these are after all the only moments of the inner argument which can be communicated. Thus the interior monologue is a convention, just as much as its ancestor, the Shakespearian soliloquy. Wolfgang Clemen says of that convention that it can 'release effects and reveal levels of existence and of inner development which could not otherwise and certainly not by a naturalistic technique be shown to us'.[3] This is also true of the interior monologue. A detailed study of the variety of its uses in the character of Julien alone would need a separate book.

Most typically, Julien's thoughts are expressed as short, quick illuminations of the narrative, admirably suited to convey the essential dynamic curiosity and restless mobility of his character. They usually reflect the way in which his perceptions are coloured by his own highly dramatized

[3] *Presidential Address of the Modern Humanities Research Association, 1964.*

view of his situation. In their simplest use they are little more than narrative devices, placed at the climax of a scene to give greater immediacy. Julien's first expressed thought—'Dieu sait ce qu'il va me faire!' (p. 17)—as his father pushes him towards the house from the sawmill, whilst giving a strong hint of their relationship, serves principally to create suspense, making explicit the question the reader should be asking himself. Sometimes this sort of attempt by Julien to interpret people and situations is much more expanded. The tenth chapter of Part II, following upon his encounter with Mathilde at the ball, consists of a whole series of interior monologues speculating on her character and leading inevitably to the vital 'M'aime-t-elle?' (p. 306) which closes the chapter. Sometimes these speculations, clouded by Julien's preconceptions, lead him comically astray, as when his excessive suspicions of the genuineness of Mathilde's distress are immediately counterpointed by a glimpse of her thoughts: 'Non! Julien ne sent rien pour moi, se disait Mathilde vraiment malheureuse' (p. 320). The relativity of human truth evident here is also seen in Julien's varying reactions to the same person at different times. His developing relationship with Madame de Rênal is punctuated by carefully differentiated judgements, gradually increasing in generous admiration as the initial social preconceptions give place to such insights of love as that which follows on the crisis of her son's illness:

> Elle a beau être noble, et moi le fils d'un ouvrier, elle m'aime. . . . Je ne suis pas auprès d'elle un valet de chambre chargé des fonctions d'amant. (p. 116)

This contrasts with his reaction to an earlier episode when her disapproving frown in response to his unusually unguarded lament for Napoleon causes him to reflect: 'Elle est bonne et douce, son goût pour moi est vif, mais elle a été élevée dans le camp ennemi' (p. 94). This reaction to a particular incident is used, as so often, to lead into a more general social comment. Especially in the early stages of the relationship, Julien's tendency to respond to every word and act in terms of class-conscious generalizations calls irresistibly to mind the conditioned reflexes of Pavlov's dogs. Madame de Rênal worries about her children being beaten: 'Quelle différence avec moi, pensa Julien. Hier encore, mon père m'a battu. Que ces gens riches sont heureux' (p. 28). Later, having offended him by offering him money to buy shirts, she tries humbly to make amends by kind attentions: 'Voilà, se disait-il, comme sont ces gens riches, ils humilient, et croient ensuite pouvoir tout réparer par quelques singeries.' (p. 39)

Sometimes his obsession with interpreting everything in social terms expands into a more detached thesis, an intellectual speculation based on general observations rather than an emotional response to a particular incident. His understanding of the motivation of his fellow-seminarists (p. 176) and his musings on the ethics of revolution and power which follow his conversation with Altamira (pp. 295-6), widely different as they are, do between them convey the dilemma of the young man who needs to find himself a place in a world which is not prepared to give him one, but who sees that the world is to be won only by a sacrifice of personal ideals to corruption, of which he is not certain of being capable. They echo two crucial monologues concerned with exposition of character which occur shortly after Julien's first appearance. The first poses the conflict between his distaste for self-abasement—'manger avec les domestiques'—and the demands of the means of his advancement to 'ce bel état de prêtre qui mène à tout' (p. 20). The second, through a clear analogy between the army under the Republic and the Church under the Restoration, explains the reasons behind his ambition and firmly reiterates his basic project—'Il faut être prêtre' (p. 24).

If the priesthood is the realm of his ambition, the army continues to provide his means and his metaphors. Even if he did not refer to his wooing of Madame de Rênal and Mathilde as campaigns, even if Stendhal did not describe him as 'l'homme malheureux en guerre avec la société', one would still have the impression that many of his interior monologues are veritable councils of war hastily convened under fire to decide on tactics (pp. 55, 66, 74, 79, 329 *et al.*). And though his thoughts sometimes reveal self-doubt (p. 75), indecision (p. 348), self-contempt (p. 358), and even despair (p. 414), he usually rallies himself with a general battle-cry—'Aux armes!' (p. 25)—or a particular watchword— 'Peu parler, peu agir' (p. 419), 'Lui faire peur' (p. 425). When self-encouragement fails, he gives himself a severe ultimatum:

Au moment précis où deux heures sonneront, j'exécuterai ce que, pendant toute la journée, je me suis promis de faire ce soir, ou je monterai chez moi me brûler la cervelle. (p. 53)

Once victory is secured, there come the self-congratulations: 'La voilà donc, cette orgueilleuse, à mes pieds' (p. 418); 'Après tout, mon roman est fini, et à moi seul tout le mérite' (p. 444). After the seduction of Madame de Rênal, he examines his performance with more detachment: 'N'ai-je manqué à rien de ce que je me dois à moi-même? Ai-je bien joué mon rôle?' (p. 87). This assessing of recent behaviour is no mere passive speculation, but becomes a kind of mental action from which the character emerges irrevocably changed, especially when, as here, it is closely associated with a monologue expressing a surprised reaction to a new experience: 'Mon Dieu! être heureux, être aimé, n'est-ce que ça?' Julien is continually pausing to take stock of his position, using his detached judgements of past actions as a basis for determining future behaviour. Such a pause, followed by a new departure, occurs in the seminary, when he realizes that until then he has merely been toying with ambition, fondly clinging to the illusion that intellectual merit alone could be a means to advancement (pp. 179–80). Moments of insight occasionally come unbidden in the midst of calm, as during the visit of Geronimo, whose untrammelled happiness makes Julien realize that he too has been happy in the unhurried solitude of his present mode of existence, prompting him to wonder with surprise: 'Le bonheur serait-il si près de moi?' (p. 154). Usually, however, insights come with the reaction to a new experience, or under the stress of emotional crisis.

It is not surprising then that the most revealing insights should come in prison after his attempt to kill Madame de Rênal. Extreme emotional pressure, a drastically new experience, and ample time to reflect—the factors combine to make Julien's radical revaluation of himself inevitable. In prison the interior monologue seems gradually to take over as the principal mode of narration; all else is an intrusion, with the exception of the visits of Madame de Rênal, to whom Julien is now so close that to talk to her is to talk to himself. The turning-point is the news that Madame de Rênal is not dead, which leads Julien to his discovery of his total loss of interest in all that has until so recently obsessed him, coupled with a first glimpse of the true nature of happiness as he experienced it at Vergy (pp. 456–7). Almost at once he contemplates suicide in a monologue which, not only in its opening—'Me tuer! Voilà la grande question' (p. 457)—but in its continuation, recalls Hamlet's most famous soliloquy, especially the lines:

> For who would bear . . .
> The oppressor's wrong, the proud man's contumely . . .
> The insolence of office . . . (*Hamlet*, Act III, Sc. 1)

Yet his refusal of suicide is still based on emulation of Napoleon rather

than on 'the dread of something after death'. This soon follows; shocked
by the sight of Chélan's decay, he begins to face the problem of his own
mortality (p. 459). The proximity of death casts a new light on everything: it gives a humble generosity to his view of other people—
Fouqué (p. 460), Mathilde (p. 462)—which in itself strengthens his
courage; it brings him a discovery of a moral sense (pp. 456, 469); it
strips away his self-dramatizing preconceptions (p. 470) to give him a
new honest lucidity (p. 473) and indifference to external circumstances
(p. 475).

This rigorous self-probing is further intensified when he is put into the
death-cell. The chapter epigraphs cease and the interior monologue
becomes a dialogue; as he comments: 'En vérité, l'homme a deux êtres
en lui' (p. 486), he seems to echo Richard II in similar circumstances:

> My brain I'll prove the female to my soul;
> My soul the father: and these two beget
> A generation of still-breeding thoughts.
> (*Richard II*, Act V, Sc. 5)

The detached observer of himself, he cuts in with a harsh joke on his
reflections on what might have been—'Pas précisément, Monsieur,
guillotiné dans trois jours' (p. 486); he finds himself quoting poetry, and
wrily comments: 'Ce sera un signe de décadence' (p. 488). Reminders of
the world outside in the persons of the priest and his father disturb his
hard-won calm, leading him to look back on his experience of that
world and to conclude despairingly that society is ruled by self-interest
and the law of the jungle (pp. 498–9). In this sombre frame of mind he
enters upon his last long monologue (pp. 499–501), reaching unsurpas-
sable depths of insight, stripping away the last layers of even involuntary
self-deception as he tortuously looks for truth—about the world, about
religion, about the human condition, and about himself, where, with a
final quiet joy of revelation, he finds it in his love for Madame de Rênal.
Reconciled with himself, he is ready to die in full self-knowledge as the
chapter ends: 'Julien se sentait fort et résolu comme l'homme qui voit
clair dans son âme' (p. 501).

After Julien, Mathilde is the character with the most interior monologues. Initially they tend to be fairly long; not having introduced her
until halfway through the novel, Stendhal cannot afford to establish her
character gradually, as he does with Julien. It is in any case appropriate

that the exposition of her character should take place principally in this way, since she has to an even greater degree than Julien the tendency to create a rich and dramatic life in her mind, but being a woman in a male-dominated society she has not the same opportunities of transferring that inner life into the world of action. The frustration of this situation sharpens the bored disgust which she feels anyway for the timorous and servile conformity of the young men of her circle, predisposing her to be interested in anyone who appears boldly different. Hence her first revealed thought is a favourable if arrogantly expressed reaction to Julien's overheard complaint of the tedium of her father's salon. 'Celui-là n'est pas né à genoux' (p. 253), she thinks, hinting immediately at a large part of her basic attitude. The rest—her desperate boredom and her efforts to escape from this through reading—is hinted at in her next monologue: 'Et pourtant j'ai dix-neuf ans! c'est l'âge du bonheur, disent tous ces nigauds à tranches dorées' (p. 281). This immediately precedes the scene of the ball, where for the first time she joins Julien at the centre of the narrative in a group of interior monologues woven around these basic themes. Through a scathing comment on her fellows (p. 285), expanded into a series of musings on the etiolating effects of civilization and inherited rank (pp. 286–8)—vividly introduced by her epigrammatic thought: 'Je ne vois que la condamnation à mort qui distingue un homme: c'est la seule chose qui ne s'achète pas' (p. 285)—her attention focuses increasingly on Julien, finally settling there with her 'O ciel! serait-il un Danton?' (p. 291).

Her next group of monologues begins with a blinding realization: 'J'ai le bonheur d'aimer' (p. 309), and proceeds with a blazing sense of release from boredom as she compares her obligatory 'grande passion' with that which she had read about in novels and in accounts of her favourite period, the late Renaissance. Over the next few pages her thoughts reveal what Stendhal later describes as 'le bonheur de se moquer de toute prudence, qui peut être si vif pour une âme ardente' (p. 468) and 'le besoin d'anxiété' which the epigraph to Chapter XII attributes to Marguerite de Valois, with whom Mathilde identifies herself. She will satisfy this need by deliberately choosing to risk her reputation and security with a man whose dynamic individualism makes him an enemy of her class. This group of monologues is Mathilde's *cristallisation* for Julien; in them she reveals the qualities she would prize in a lover, and persuades herself that Julien has them. The next small group results from her doubt of this. Beginning again with a plain enunciation of the

theme—'Peut-être aussi n'a-t-il que les apparences d'un homme
supérieur' (p. 326)—she again bases her reflections on a nostalgic comparison with the days of Henri III (p. 327), and expresses the ultimate
resource of her self-sufficiency by a literary allusion: 'Eh bien! je me
dirai comme Médée: *Au milieu de tant de périls il me reste MOI*' (p. 328).

Her preoccupations established and the intrigue with Julien launched,
Mathilde's interior monologues become sparser and shorter. Her reactions to the fulfilment of her fantasies when Julien comes to her bedroom
pass quickly from triumphant relief—'Ah! que cet homme est digne de
tout mon amour!' (p. 339)—through solemn realization—'Il est donc
mon maître' (p. 341)—and comic formality—'Il faut cependant que
je lui parle, cela est dans les convenances, on parle à son amant' (p. 341)—
to doubting disappointment—'Me serais-je trompée, n'aurais-je pas
d'amour pour lui?' (p. 343). This question will preoccupy both Mathilde
and Julien for some time, and though she will sometimes experience
indifference towards him (p. 400), she will always return to an extreme
self-abandonment (p. 401), and her attitude to the relationship will continue to be characterized by a sense of her duty to be extraordinary
(p. 353) and a melodramatic delight in the excitement of her situation
(pp. 347, 349), culminating in the horrified joy with which she looks
forward to her own heroic part in Julien's condemnation and execution
(p. 471).

Madame de Rênal's thoughts all relate to Julien and her love for him;
even her shrewd reflections on the means of deceiving her husband
(pp. 127–8) are chiefly a measure of Stendhal's view of the power of love
to transform character. All her thoughts about Julien are generous,
outward-looking, self-effacing. Her shocked displeasure at his clumsy
attempt to kiss her in public is quickly and happily dispersed: 'C'est la
timidité de l'amour dans un homme d'esprit' (p. 82). A touching worry
about her age contrasts poignantly with the immediately preceding note
of Julien's wish to appear experienced (p. 88). In her longest monologue,
just before Julien's departure from Verrières, she hypothesizes with
dread on his behaviour once he has gone, but ends by humbly blaming
herself (p. 156).

Of the three central characters, Madame de Rênal has by far the fewest
interior monologues. This does not mean that she is the least important,
nor that she has no inner life; it simply means that she is transparent, that
Stendhal has no need to show us her thoughts because they are artlessly

betrayed in her every action. She has nothing to hide, and yet for a long time, she remains mysterious for Julien, because he is unable to categorize her according to his preconceptions. Such preconceptions as she has yield without a struggle when new experience proves them false. Both she and Julien approach their vital first meeting outside the Rênal house (I, Ch. 6) with trepidation; he expects to find a haughty lady of the manor, she a rough brute who will beat her children. The agreeable unexpectedness of the reality causes both to behave with more intimate spontaneity than they might otherwise have shown at a first meeting. Julien spends the rest of the novel painfully rediscovering the value of that privileged moment; she never loses her intuitive recognition of the true nature of 'le chemin qui mène au bonheur'.

The Marquis de la Mole provides the perfect example of the use of the interior monologue for a major secondary character. Used selectively along with other techniques, it highlights their effects and shows us the hero through another consciousness whose own limitations and motivations are clear. Moreover, a distinct and consistent development is seen in the thoughts, which provide a shorthand guide to the relationship. The first three monologues (pp. 241–2) show the Marquis's disappointment with his new secretary; his bad spelling makes him doubt his vaunted ability. Later the same evening, after Julien's good performance at dinner, the Marquis wonders with comic astonishment: 'Serait-il possible qu'il sût quelque chose?' (p. 244). His next short monologue finds him more benignly disposed, lucidly remarking on Julien's unusual lack of awe before the *grand monde* (pp. 273–4). One line later comes a frank admission of his attachment to Julien, but any possibility of a sentimental reaction from the reader is forestalled by the patronizing comparison of this attachment with that of a dog-lover, and the equally patronizing thought that he will leave Julien a bauble in his will (p. 274). By the next page, some time has passed, and the relationship has progressed to genuine respect and the confidence in Julien's ability which will enable the Marquis to entrust him first with a mission to London, and then—the summit of Julien's diplomatic career—with the Secret Note. As this latter mission begins (p. 371), the Marquis, in his longest monologue so far, puts Julien's ability above that of his son, who would be able to do no more than die well. At the thought that Julien too might know how to die well, Stendhal vividly implies the depths which the Marquis's affection has now reached by abruptly breaking off to launch without transition into his 'Montons en voiture'. This is the climax of the Marquis's respect and affection for Julien. The next time we see his thoughts directly, his world has been overturned by the news of Mathilde's pregnancy. In his agitation, he clutches at straw after straw, finally retreating into the attitudes of his caste and generation (p. 438). The paternal idyll with Julien is shattered; threatened closer to home, he wishes momentarily for Julien's death (p. 439). Ultimately, a less violent mood prevails, and in his last monologue—by far the most extended— the final synthesis is made of the insights which the relationship has given him into Julien's character (pp. 442–3).

TYPES AND CARICATURES

Flat characters, sometimes called types, are constructed round a single idea or quality; when there is more than one factor in them, we get the beginning of the curve towards the round. (E. M. Forster)

There can be a hyperselective use of these techniques for purposes of satire. Overcharging and simplification of the character produces the impression of mechanistic behaviour, of creatures of society trapped in their prejudices. Sometimes this effect is obtained by allowing one interior monologue to capture the essence of the character's attitude. Croisenois, for instance, is much mentioned but scarcely exists as a solid figure. He fits perfectly into his background and in many ways represents it—well-bred, perfectly brave, perfectly dull, with above all a respect for convention and, as his monologue shows (p. 286), a consequent fearful mistrust of *singularité*. Though this highly selective use of the interior monologue conveys the essence of the minor characters—Korasoff's francophile dandyism (p. 394), Beauvoisis's sartorial obsession (p. 267), even the respectful vacuity of the Marquis de la Mole (p. 245)—its effect is not altogether caricatural; allowing even one glimpse of their minds is unusual enough to unsettle our fixed notions of character. We feel we may be given another, more profound, more disturbing, as indeed we are with Monsieur de Rênal (pp. 123–7).

The real method of caricature is through first impressions. The Bishop of Agde remains forever fixed in his vain self-benediction; Chas-Bernard will be forever fussing over his precious decorations. To be more precise, since all the characters are initially presented in a way which epitomizes them, caricature is achieved simply by not developing that first impression. The major characters are caricatures until Stendhal chooses to develop them; conversely, one feels that he always could develop the minor ones if he chose to do so. Indeed, although there is a clear hierarchy of characterization, it is impossible to draw a sharp dividing line between characters and caricatures. There is a possibility of movement either way. Monsieur de Rênal hovers between a mimetic and a satirical presentation, particularly through the long interior monologue in which Stendhal leads him along a tightrope between pathos and absurdity as he broods on the anonymous letter. Even without this, one feels that, compared with Valenod, he has the saving grace of imagination, albeit one which moves in restricted circles. Croisenois too, shadowy as he is, can be made to achieve a new stature by dying in a duel in defence of Mathilde's honour, as a prelude to Julien's execution (p. 503). Sometimes the development happens the other way; when a character is under stress, he may clutch at his *idées reçues* and his social role as a lifebelt. The Marquis retreats into his authority, Mathilde into her arrogance, Pirard into his austerity. When the characters move in this way, it means either that they fix themselves, or free themselves from their former immobility. Either way, it is their freedom that is in question.

Even the hero is not exempt from this possibility. Not only is he used as a satirical agent; he is also himself an object of satire. On many occasions Stendhal is mocking him as a prisoner of his obsessions and preconceptions. Indeed, the whole of his behaviour, up to his discovery of self in prison, can be seen as mechanistic and therefore presented in a satirical light. This impression is reinforced when we consider that the only major character who is never satirically presented—with whom indeed Stendhal takes great pains to avoid any suspicion of irony—is Madame de Rênal, who in the final section of the novel is the main agent and embodiment of the true values which the hero finally discovers.

3. Meanings

It is first of all the author's attitude that is narrated, though in that attitude there be implied a whole experience and a theory of life. (R. L. Stevenson)

The conflict of values with which *Le Rouge* is concerned is expressed by reference of the characters' behaviour to external patterns, either historical or literary in their source. Archetypally opposed answers are provided to the problem posed by the conception of life as a search—*la recherche du bonheur*; this is the basis both of characterization and of the structure of values. The search for happiness in *Le Rouge* begins in the public world, in the realm of society and politics, manifesting itself as ambition, and ends in the private world, in solitude, in prison, in the inner life of memory and imagination, manifesting itself as love and ultimately becoming equated with the search for self-knowledge. At the same time, the conflict persists to the very end of the novel, where we see the old values still clung to by Mathilde, and the new discovered by Julien and embodied in Madame de Rênal—as they have been throughout the novel for the reader, though not for the hero. The significance of the two heroines is therefore to represent not only two different sorts of love, not only two social classes, but also the two conflicting sets of values with which the hero is faced.

The principal model for Julien is of course Napoleon; he is the most recent archetype of the public solution to the *recherche du bonheur*, representing the unscrupulous egoistical ambition through which Julien seeks initially to find happiness. Once he has chosen this way, to succeed becomes not only a need, but a duty. The word *devoir* is constantly uppermost in his mind; he has surrendered his freedom of action and must refer all decisions about his conduct to the central control of the Napoleon myth. The idea of *devoir* has not just a socio-political motivation; it is also a personal ideal. Julien's need is to prove himself, to succeed in difficult self-imposed tasks in order to cultivate his will-power, to discover his strength and to free himself from the power of circumstance, which he must do if he is not to despise himself. For a long time the search for self-knowledge is inseparable from the troublesome need for self-esteem, which is uneasily dependent on the esteem of everybody else. So uncertain is Julien of himself that he is hypersensitive to the opinions not only of those he respects, such as Pirard and the Marquis de la Mole, but also of those whom, intellectually, he despises, for instance the guests at Valenod's dinner-party. Even at the end, when he has become emotionally self-sufficient, he is concerned to die well and give no handle for contempt. This concern for the opinion of others is an important motivating force for Julien's actions, irrespective of social considerations, although often associated with them. He is always aware of his social inferiority, but in the two love-affairs which constitute his major attacks upon the class-structure, Julien is no Joe Lampton,[1] attempting to climb over class-barriers to win social rewards. This is the result, but the motive, disinterested in material terms, is much more radical and revolutionary —to overthrow the barriers, to nullify them, to deny the system of values which they defend. The worldly rewards come as an accidental bonus. The real reward for Julien is that he has bolstered his ego by proving himself personally equal, indeed superior, to his social superiors.

Thus, in so far as Stendhal sympathizes with this aspect of Julien's behaviour and is concerned with political ideals, it is *liberté* rather than *égalité* that he is proposing—not democracy, but the aristocracy of personal merit based on fearless individualism which is constantly in evidence in his conception of sixteenth-century Italy, notably in the comments on the chronicle which was to serve as model for *La Chartreuse de Parme*:

> C'est qu'alors on n'estimait dans un homme que ce qui lui est personnel, et ce n'était pas une qualité personnelle que d'être comme tout le monde. (*Mélanges de Littérature*, I, p. 278)

It is precisely because Julien is not 'comme tout le monde' that Mathilde chooses to make him her lover; he has the dynamic individualism which the young men of her own class lack. Sharing with Julien the obsession with a personal myth to guide her behaviour, she much more consciously abandons the protection of the class-structure and creates her own superiority by a free act of will. In fact, she is never able to forget her inherited superiority, and the resulting tension in her is one cause of the neurotic instability of their relationship. Yet immense courage and self-sufficiency are shown by her wilful complicity with this frightening stranger, to whom she attributes the character of Danton, the

[1] The hero of John Braine's *Room at the Top*.

arch-bogeyman of her class. In doing this, she is updating her ruling myth of her ancestor, Boniface de la Mole, executed for his part in a rebellious conspiracy. Significantly, the past she lives in is the sixteenth century, when the world was young, and when, having no inherited laurels to rest on, men worth the name had to create their own superiority, valuing life less than personal glory. This is Stendhal's view of the six-teenth century; it is also that of Mathilde, who, in the drama she creates of her life, casts Julien as Boniface and herself as his mistress, Marguerite de Navarre.

This is a further cause of discord; for Julien, in the drama he creates of his life, casts himself as the *plébéien révolté*. Mathilde's role is freely chosen out of boredom, whereas Julien's is imposed upon him by neces-sity, a destiny which, however mistakenly, he does not feel free to refuse. The other roles which he adopts in the course of the novel are con-sciously assumed masks used for a purpose, ready to be discarded when they have served that purpose. He is very uncertain whether he is really a Don Juan, but he thinks, mistakenly, that he needs to appear so for the purpose of seducing Madame de Rênal. Even more fundamentally, he has no natural gift for the role of Tartuffe, the most significant of his utility roles. Julien makes the arch-hypocrite his principal role because he judges, from his little experience of the world, that hypocrisy is its typical mode of behaviour and hence the way to success, but also because he needs to protect both his disreputable political views and his extreme sensitivity from prying eyes. To say the opposite of what he feels becomes axiomatic. There is a sense of vulnerability, a need to show nothing of himself, a fear of ridicule or worse if he should betray his real feelings. This self-protective obsession reaches its greatest intensity in his dealings with Mathilde. On her side, the same reluctance to reveal herself indicates a fear of abandoning self-sufficiency, a refusal to love as Madame de Rênal does, with a complete and unregretted surrender of pride and privacy.

Madame de Rênal is sincere and unashamed with Julien because she is free. Only once does she lose her freedom and succumb under great stress to the petty chicanery of her society—in the letter to the Marquis de la Mole—and the drastic unexpectedness of this lapse is one cause of Julien's subsequent rage. Apart from this, she is unquestionably the principal repository of the author's values. She attains the ideal of self-knowledge intuitively once she is transformed by love; she gives love pride of place in her scale of values; she loves Julien for himself, seeing him as he really is, knowing him long before he knows himself because she considers people as individual human-beings and not as actors in a drama which she has already written. She lacks too the petty vices which her husband embodies—vanity, and the fear of public opinion. Her only fear is of divine punishment, and she braves this with a minimum of hesitation; once committed, she does not look back. Above all, she lives, not in a nostalgically viewed past, nor in a grandiosely hypothetical future, but in the present, where she accepts such happiness as each moment brings, fluidly adjusting her hopes to her experience, not without anguish but without fear and compromise. She is thus a touchstone by which we may judge other characters, especially Julien and Mathilde. Doing so, we see that their habit of approaching experience in the shadow of a preconceived ideal, whilst providing them with an incentive to embark upon unusual and liberating behaviour, ultimately hinders personal fulfilment. These values can only provide the initial impetus; once launched, the character must jettison them if he is to rise to the level of Madame de Rênal. Mathilde proves unable to do so. Her myth remains with her when it is no longer relevant to the situation, impeding her progress towards self-knowledge, fixing her in a futile repetition of more and more extravagant gestures which appear more and more devoid of meaning, both to the hero and to the reader.

Julien too is continually reaching a point beyond which the author's sympathy ceases. This happens whenever his obsession with *devoir* gets in the way of his *chasse au bonheur*. This obsession certainly helps him in the short term to win the fruits of success, but in the longer term it prevents him from enjoying them. Above all, it acts as a barrier between him and the happiness which Madame de Rênal offers, and by the same token bars his way to self-knowledge. Stendhal is continually debunking Julien's tendency to self-dramatization, his cult of *devoir*, his worship of Napoleon, and in general his literary-based preconceptions about experience. Thus he is doing what Cervantes did some two hundred years earlier in *Don Quixote*, and what Flaubert was to do less than thirty years later in *Madame Bovary*. There are of course differences. All three writers use comic means to lay bare the self-deception at the heart of the central character, but where Cervantes calls into question the whole nature of reality by setting against the Don's gradual loss of idealism a contrary development on the part of Sancho Panza, and where Flaubert leaves Emma in a barren world reduced to its basic elements of physical functioning and the bitter triumph of self-interest and pragmatic stupidity,

Stendhal on the other hand, having overthrown Julien's first myth, replaces it by an even more idealized conception of the world. Not only does he overthrow Julien's first set of values, but he does so gratuitously; he first allows his hero to succeed according to those values, thus rendering his subsequent rejection of them more striking. To reject the world because he had played it at its own game and lost would make Julien at best pitiable; to beat it and retire to live on his winnings would make him possibly enviable, but by no means admirable; to beat it and then throw his winnings in its face makes him heroic. And, like a hero, having attained one unattainable goal, he then attains another— oblivion of the world in the perfection of love, inextricably associated with the total happiness of perfect self-knowledge in the solitude of prison.

The prison-chapters are the key to the meaning of the whole novel, whose constant movement inwards must logically culminate in romance, in the study of the hero *in vacuo*. In a sense, we have seen Julien *in vacuo* throughout, partly through the emphasis laid on his alienation from the rest of society, partly through his position as the central consciousness in the narration. A full and final revelation of that consciousness requires a solitary setting where the hero may look lucidly at himself and at the world which has for so long been his battlefield and which has just witnessed his overthrow at the height of victory.

DÉNOUEMENT

A story must convey a sense of inevitability: that which happens in it must seem to be the only thing that could have happened. (Ford Madox Ford)

The manner of Julien's overthrow has provoked considerable discussion[2] which has centred on three points: the supposed implausibility of the Marquis de la Mole's reaction to Madame de Rênal's letter; the supposed implausibility of Julien's reaction; the speeding up of the narrative at the crucial moment, with its consequent telescoping of time and lack of explanation of Julien's thoughts.

All these points can be answered. What has already been shown of the Marquis's relationship with Julien provides a firm enough background for an explanation of his reaction. Moreover, if we look more closely at

[2] For a survey of this, and a closely argued interpretation, see D. J. Mossop's article *Julien Sorel, the Vulgar Assassin*, in *French Studies* (1969), pp. 138–44.

his final monologue (p. 442), we can see how, taking stock of Julien as his worldly career approaches its end, Stendhal specifically prepares us for the Marquis's reaction and anticipates his critics' interpretations of Julien's motivation, asking their questions and providing his answers. This crucial inner debate of the Marquis might be expressed thus:

Question: Is not Julien brilliantly astute?

Answer: Yes, but there is something mysterious and frightening about him. In any case, his astuteness is only evident in impersonal matters; in judging his own situation in society, he overlooks the crucial factor—the need for support—preferring to remain a lone wolf. Therefore he has not the slow cunning of a social climber.

Question: To judge by his conversation, is he not cynically cold and dispassionate?

Answer: Perhaps this is a defence to keep his passions in check, a deliberate discipline and suppression of natural impulses.

Question: Is there nothing certain and irreducible about his character?

Answer: He cannot bear contempt.

Conclusion: He will react spontaneously and reveal the truth of the enigma only under the pressure of extreme contempt, or what he interprets as contempt, from someone whose opinion is important to him. This pressure will come from both the Marquis and Madame de Rênal on the issue raised at the end of the monologue—whether Julien's love for Mathilde is genuine or merely a vulgar means of advancement.

Thus Stendhal indicates in advance that Julien's behaviour will have the same basic motive as all his other actions so far, a hypersensitivity to contempt so obsessive as to merit the name of a passion, which causes its sufferer to judge everything with his imagination in its own terms and hence to dramatize his own situation and behaviour, suspending his normal perception of the world around him. It is pertinent to note a comment which Berlioz makes in his account of the incident in his own life referred to earlier:

> Les gens passionnés sont charmants, ils s'imaginent tous que le monde entier est préoccupé de leur passion quelle qu'elle soit, et ils mettent une bonne foi vraiment édifiante à se conformer à cette opinion. (Berlioz, *Mémoires*, Ch. 34)

Passion always more or less blinds the hero to other interpretations of a situation; at moments of stress it does so most intensively, concentrating all his attention on its object; everything except the achievement of its ends is as if non-existent. Julien always judges and perceives in terms of his project; here his project is short-term and all-absorbing. He can literally think of nothing else.

Perhaps he cannot even think. An even more revealing layer of personality than thought is the subconscious. The word, not being current in Stendhal's time, is never used by him, but the idea is. In 1822, with his knack of turning all branches of learning to the service of 'la connaissance du cœur humain', he wrote a short essay entitled *Le Caractère et la Géologie*, in which he demonstrates how vegetal deposits may cover a sub-stratum of granite, making it appear to the untrained eye as a smooth and almost unbroken plain, when it is in reality very jagged, with soaring peaks and plunging precipices. He then establishes an analogy with character, using words which might have been written with Julien in mind:

> Le granit, c'est le caractère naturel d'un homme, sa manière habituelle de chercher le bonheur. . . . Le remplissage, c'est ce que la politesse, l'usage du monde, la prudence, fait sur un caractère. (*Mélanges de Littérature*, II, p. 197)

He continues by saying that a man may well assume his surface behaviour to be the reality of his character until, under the pressure of 'grandes circonstances', the hard bedrock will be unexpectedly revealed with precipices he had never dreamed of. He cites Cassio's seemingly uncharacteristic violence in Act II, Scene 3 of *Othello*. It is easy to see how this analogy can be applied to the novel as a means of characterization through behaviour, especially critical behaviour such as Julien's shooting of Madame de Rênal. Indeed, since the search for happiness in *Le Rouge* becomes the search for self-knowledge, this revelation of the subconscious through action is perhaps the method of characterization towards which the whole novel ultimately tends. To misquote Lewis Carroll: 'How do I know what I am until I see what I do?'

Such behaviour cannot by its nature be too obviously prepared by the author, nor can he be very explicit about it. He cannot explain what is *a priori* inexplicable without robbing it of its naturalness and hence its plausibility; if it is subconscious, it is beyond words. He can only show it, explain around it by a subtle and at the time unnoticed accumulation of clues, retreating at the crucial moment into silence and narration by omission. The clues in Julien's earlier behaviour are the very fabric of his character. Most important are the occasions when, thinking himself

insulted, he is seized by an obsessive rage: Madame de Rênal's offer of money for buying shirts (p. 38), her husband's incessant slights, the incident with Amanda Binet's lover (pp. 164–6) or the Comte de Beauvoisis's coachman (p. 265), and—most relevant of all—Mathilde's 'J'ai horreur de m'être livrée au premier venu' (p. 346), to which Julien replies unreflectively by seizing her father's sword as if to kill her.

As the Marquis rightly divines, Julien's career has been one long suppression of passion; on occasions such as these we see it bursting through. Most of the time we have seen it controlled and channelled into activities which are not likely to lead to happiness. The subduing of Mathilde leads possibly to the joy of conquest, but certainly not to happiness. 'J'ai su me faire aimer de ce monstre d'orgueil' (p. 444)—these are not the words of a happy man. Julien's energy has been constantly misdirected; far from dissipating his passion, the activities he has chosen increase the underlying feeling of frustration, which must sooner or later find an outlet in a veritable explosion[3] of the whole personality. There is such a drastic reversal of values in Julien after the shooting that it is futile to isolate it and examine it within its own narrow perspective. It only makes sense if we look at it from the end of the novel and take into account everything that has gone before. Yet even in the chapters immediately preceding we can see how Stendhal has prepared us for the event, by reporting the thoughts of the Marquis, by shifting the emphasis on to other characters and on to bustling plot business, by speeding up and lightening the narrative, and so generally detaching us from Julien. Nowhere are we at a greater distance from him than at the moment of his worldly success. The delight in his conquest of Mathilde, in his acquisition of wealth, an aristocratic name and a commission, is Julien's delight; it is not the author's, nor is it the reader's. We feel—as we are meant to feel—that these rewards are won, so contemptuously easily, by artificial means, and we no longer recognise Julien as he wins them. He is at the furthest pole from self-knowledge and from freedom, and hence from the right to our admiration. He must now either win our respect by an irrevocable leap in the least expected direction to a final shock of self-discovery or, retaining the planifying accretions of corruption and worldliness, sink into the oblivion of the false and the commonplace, remaining undiscovered both to himself and to us, and so disappointing all the expectations we have legitimately acquired throughout the novel.

[3] Or, to change metaphors, a storm; the relevant chapter is entitled *Un Orage*.

DISCOVERY

The only general attribute of romance is the fact of the kind of experience with which it deals—experience liberated and operating in a medium which relieves it of the inconvenience of a state subject to all our vulgar communities. (Henry James)

Fortunately, Stendhal does not disappoint us. He leads his hero through his material downfall to his moral salvation, delivering him from the false image he has created of himself. With the news of Madame de Rênal's survival, Julien grows tired of playing at heroes and is able to come to a true estimate of himself, to rediscover his innocence and so to die at peace. *Le Rouge* is finally a tragedy, for the hero is brought to his ruin through the essential flaw in his nature, and this flaw—imagination —is also a virtue for which we admire him more. Moreover, the downfall brings the hero's purgation from his faults, revealing to him the true nature of his affections. Julien's reconciliation with Madame de Rênal, and with himself through the recognition of his responsibility, has a Shakespearian quality; the climax comes not in the violence of passion, but in the calm after the storm, in the lucid silence of the prison-cell.

Even here Julien is not entirely free from society's corrupting touch. Frilair's machinations, Mathilde's histrionics, his father's visit, the priest outside in the rain, the confessor who tries to persuade him to a propagandist conversion—these among others are further tests which he must endure before winning the right to his peace of mind. He remains untouched, thanks to the strength he draws from his new happiness with Madame de Rênal, thanks above all to his rigorous intellectual purity which will now allow no hypocrisy, not even towards himself. Julien now is a puritan in the same sense as Shakespeare's Coriolanus, exiled because he cannot submit to the ritual humiliation which society requires as its homage. Julien is unable to debase himself, to destroy his hard-won integrity by pandering to the sensibilities of society any longer. He has several chances of trying to save himself from execution, but he chooses to die. In his speech to the jury (p. 482) he throws away the mask he has worn for so long, and he cannot bring himself to pick it up again. He is intensely aware that the individual who will be completely true to himself must be alienated from society. The superiority of his moral isolation is sharply symbolized by his physical situation in a cell at the top of the citadel, as it was earlier in the novel in the mountains on the way to visit Fouqué or in his seminary-cell with its commanding view.

The monastic overtones evident in the contemplative life which Julien now leads are by no means contradicted by his other source of consolation—the completely shared love, free from all deceptions, which he and Madame de Rênal enjoy. Indeed, it enhances them, rendered precarious and perfect as it is by its severe limitations in duration and continuity. Even without the visits of Madame de Rênal, Julien would be happier in prison than at any other point in the novel,[4] but this discovery of love comes as a crowning joy. Throughout the novel re-echoes the 'N'est-ce que ça?' which Julien utters immediately after his first experience of physical love with Madame de Rênal, expressing the recurrent disappointment with experience of the person who dreams about life before living it. Here at last Julien, though again surprised, is not disappointed by the marvellously unspectacular discovery that happiness gives life its value and comes when least expected. It comes only when he is unwatched, away from the world, as it came unvalued at Vergy when, chasing butterflies with Madame de Rênal, 'loin des regards des hommes . . . il se livrait au plaisir d'exister' (p. 50). He discovers that the happiness of love is not the turbulent ecstasy imagined by him and Mathilde, but a very quiet matter, characterized particularly by 'un extrême sérieux', as Stendhal says in *De l'Amour* (Ch. 33). It is the peaceful gravity of two people sharing the complete trust of intense friendship elevated by passion and isolated in time and space. It is in short an impossible happiness and a very idealized world that Stendhal moves his hero into at the end, but rendered plausible by being quite literally removed from the everyday world of contacts and consequences in which the novel has previously moved. The total perspective is given by the closing chapters, and the novel as a whole is seen to follow a traditional pattern whereby the hero passes through a series of tests in the world, in which he must succeed in order to prove himself worthy of the reward of retreat from the world into his private happiness and peace of mind.[5]

Thus *Le Rouge* contains elements of traditional myths, elements of the archetypal novel, elements of satire, elements of tragedy. These latter are further evident in the use which Stendhal makes of certain characters to show the hero the ways of the world. He, in the final analysis, is unworldly; this is what makes him a hero. He does not coolly examine the

[4] For a development of this point, see Henry Amer's article *Amour, Prison et Temps chez Stendhal*, in *Nouvelle Revue Française* (1962), pp. 483–90.

[5] For a development of this idea see *Le décor mythique de La Chartreuse de Parme* by Gilbert Durand (Paris, J. Corti, 1961).

world, he is unable to perceive the importance of petty details, as is made particularly clear in the seminary episode. Instead, he judges everything with his imagination—as Stendhal says, adding: 'Cette erreur est d'un homme supérieur' (p. 358). So he is provided with mentors to initiate him into the world and show him its workings. Most of them are older than he is—Chélan, the chirurgien-major, Pirard, the Marquis de la Mole, Madame de Rênal—providing a subsidiary theme of youth and experience; some are his own age—Fouqué, Korasoff, Beauvoisis, Norbert de la Mole; all, with the exception of Madame de Rênal, although in varying degrees sympathetic to him, sooner or later fail to understand him, as Oenone fails to understand Phèdre, as the Nurse fails to understand Juliet, as the sympathetic onlooker always reaches a point beyond which he is incapable of understanding the tragic hero exalted by passion and, through his bafflement, serves further to enhance the hero's moral isolation.